コア表現リスト　リーディング編

Reading

1	Be sure to ～	必ず～してください
2	I / We suggest that you ～	～することを提案します
3	I am / We are happy to inform you that ～	～をお知らせすることをうれしく思います
4	I / We recommend that you ～	～することを推奨します
5	update ～	～を更新します
6	I am writing to ～ / about ～	～するために / ～の件でお便りしています
7	Please note that ～	～にご注意ください
8	I would appreciate it if you could ～	～していただけるとありがたく思います
9	be required to ～	～することが求められます
10	I / We look forward to ～	～を楽しみにしています
11	I'd like to call / draw your attention to ～	～に注目してください
12	Should 主語＋動詞～ , please ～	万が一～の場合は、～してください
13	be encouraged to ～	～することが推奨されます
14	Please take a moment to ～	お手数ですが、～するようお願いします

No.1 ～ 7　ほぼ確実に設問の正答箇所となる
No.8 ～ 14　非常に高い確率で設問の正答箇所となる

AN AMAZING AVENUE FOR THE TOEIC® L&R TEST 400

頻出表現と頻出単語でつかむ TOEIC® L&R TEST 400点

Hiromi Hagi
Adelia Falk
Minako Fukui
Keiichi Eto
Takako Ramsden
Naoko Kaneda
Makoto Kurata

photographs by

iStockphoto

音声ファイルのダウンロード／ストリーミング

CD マーク表示がある箇所は、音声を弊社 HP より無料でダウンロード／ストリーミングすることができます。トップページのバナーをクリックし、書籍検索してください。書籍詳細ページに音声ダウンロードアイコンがございますのでそちらから自習用音声としてご活用ください。

TESTUDY

本書ではTESTUDY（＝TEST＋STUDY）という「e-Learning＋オンラインテスト」システムがご利用いただけます。各Unitの復習として、e-Learningやオンラインテストが受験できます。全て教員の指示に従って学習・受験してください。

※本サービスは教育機関におけるクラス単位でのご利用に限らせていただきます。

AN AMAZING AVENUE FOR THE TOEIC® L&R TEST 400

頻出表現と頻出単語でつかむ TOEIC® L&R TEST 400 点

はしがき

本書の特徴は、独自の手法で選出したTOEIC® Listening & Reading Test（以下TOEIC L&Rテストと称する）のデータを最大限に活かしていることです。本書の姉妹書である『An Amazing Approach to the TOEIC® L&R Test』でも取り上げたように、TOEIC® L&R Testには、頻出の語彙・表現に一定のパターンがあります。ビジネスシーンで頻出する表現　Why don't you 〜 や Be sure to 〜 などは、それに続く内容の情報価値が高く、TOEIC® L&Rテストで非常に高い確率で設問の正答箇所になることがあります。本書では、難易度の高い表現ではなく、初学習者でも比較的覚えやすく、かつTOEIC® L&Rテストにて頻出するものを厳選して「コア表現」と名付けました。本書で扱う「コア表現」にはListeningとReadingで合計28表現（各14表現）を選び、すべてのユニットで何度も繰り返し模擬問題で学習することで定着を目指すアプローチをとっています。そうすることでTOEIC® L&Rテストのスコアアップを狙います。また、各ユニットではトピック別に学習ができ、その分野の頻出単語についても、独自のデータ選出法にて実際にテストに頻出する10語を厳選・精査して、模擬英文と設問を作成しました。コア表現と頻出単語の相乗効果で英語を聞く力、読む力の基礎力を身につけることができます。さらに、各ユニットにて必ず押さえたい重要ポイントをLet's Learn!で解説しています。

本書で学習することで、TOEIC® L&Rテストの基礎固めだけでなく、英語の基礎的な能力向上を目指します。学習者の皆さんが、英語の総合基礎能力を身につけ、今後のさらなる学習へ進んでいかれることがあれば、著者陣にとって、これ以上の喜びはありません。

最後に、本書を刊行するにあたり、株式会社 成美堂の田村栄一氏、佐野泰孝氏には、きわめて細やかなご配慮、そして、編集面で的確なご助言をいただきました。ここに感謝の意を表させていただきます。

2023年　盛夏

著者一同

本書の構成と使い方

本書は、全ユニットがTOEIC® L&R Testに頻出するトピック別に構成されています。各ユニットのPart 1からPart 7までの練習問題には独自の方法で選出した10単語と、28のコア表現が使用されています。学習した単語は以後のユニットにも使われ、繰り返しふれることで復習することができます。各ユニットは8ページからなり、以下の内容で構成されています。

【各ユニットの構成】

1. トピック

2. Word Bank

3. Listening Section

- Let's Learn!（Part 1-4のうち2つのパート）

- Let's Try!（Part 1-4）

4. Reading Section

- Let's Learn!（Part 5-7のうち2つのパート）

- Let's Try!（Part 5-7）

1. トピック

そのユニットでどのようなトピックを学ぶのかを確認します。

2. Word Bank

トピックに関する頻出単語をイラストと結びつけます。音声とともにしっかりと学べます。

3. Let's Learn!

そのユニットで特に焦点を置きたい重要ポイントと解法のヒントがまとめてあります。取り上げるパートは「本書のターゲット（p.6-7）」に記載されています。また、Let's Try! の問題の一部分を予備演習に使っています。

4. Let's Try!

実際のTOEIC® L&Rテストと同じ形式で、各ユニットのトピックに合った問題の練習をすることができます。練習問題には、Word Bankで練習した単語とコア表現、そして、Let's Learn! で学んだポイントが含まれています。Part 1から7まで通して練習することで、ユニット毎にTOEIC® L&Rテストの疑似体験ができることを目的としています。

TOEIC® Listening & Reading Test の問題形式

リスニングセクション（約45分―100問）

パート	パート名	問題数
1	写真描写問題	6
2	応答問題	25
3	会話問題	39
4	説明文問題	30

リーディングセクション（75分―100問）

パート	パート名	問題数
5	短文穴埋め問題	30
6	長文穴埋め問題	16
7	1つの文書	29
	複数の文書	25

☺ Part 1　とはどんなパート？　<写真描写問題>

1つの写真に対し、4つの説明文が放送されます。写真の内容を最も適切に描写しているものを選びます。

☺ Part 2　とはどんなパート？　<応答問題>

1つの質問または発言と、それに対する3つの応答を聞き、最も適切な応答を選びます。

☺ Part 3　とはどんなパート？　<会話問題>

会話と会話に対する3つの設問が放送されます。設問は問題用紙にも印刷されています。各設問に対する最も適切なものを選択肢から選びます。

☺ Part 4　とはどんなパート？　<説明文問題>

電話メッセージ、お知らせなどの説明文と設問が放送されます。設問は問題用紙にも印刷されています。各設問に対する最も適切なものを選択肢から選びます。

☺ Part 5　とはどんなパート？　<短文穴埋め問題>

4つの選択肢から空所に入る最も適切なものを選び、不完全な文を完成させます。

☺ Part 6　とはどんなパート？　<長文穴埋め問題>

4つの選択肢から空所に入る最も適切なものを選び、不完全な文書を完成させます。

☺ Part 7　とはどんなパート？　<読解問題>

さまざまな内容や形式の1つ、または複数の文書に関しての設問が出題され、4つの選択肢から最も適切なものを選びます。

本書のターゲット　Let's Learn! のトピック

	Part 1 (写真描写問題)	Part 2 (応答問題)	Part 3 (会話問題)	Part 4 (説明文問題)
	Part 1とはどんなパート	Part 2とはどんなパート	Part 3とはどんなパート	Part 4とはどんなパート
Unit 1 **Restaurants**	写真に写っているものに注目〈人〉	さまざまな疑問文		
Unit 2 **Daily Life**		疑問詞を使った疑問文	設問の特徴	
Unit 3 **Campus Life**	写真に写っているものに注目〈もの〉			トークの種類
Unit 4 **Shopping**		Yes / No 疑問文	森問題と木問題	
Unit 5 **Entertainment**	写真に写っているものに注目〈風景〉			トークの種類〈ラジオ放送〉
Unit 6 **Office Work (1)**		選択疑問文	森問題〈話題〉	
Unit 7 **Office Work (2)**	位置を表す語(句)			トークの種類〈会議の一部①〉
Unit 8 **Bank & Post office**		付加疑問文	森問題〈職業〉	
Unit 9 **Job Hunting**		平叙文		トークの種類〈電話メッセージ〉
Unit 10 **Housing**	人物の行動を表す動詞		森問題〈場所〉	
Unit 11 **Transportation**		依頼・申し出		トークの種類〈アナウンス〉
Unit 12 **Hotels**		提案・勧誘	木問題	
Unit 13 **Events**	受動態			トークの種類〈会議の一部②〉
Unit 14 **Health**		同じ発音・似た発音の語（句）	図表問題	

Part 5 (短文穴埋め問題)	**Part 6** (長文穴埋め問題)	**Part 7** (読解問題)
Part 5とはどんなパート	Part 6とはどんなパート	Part 7とはどんなパート
文の構造 〈主語(S)と述語動詞(V)〉	文書の種類	
名詞		文書の種類〈アンケート調査〉
形容詞		文書の種類 〈テキストメッセージ〉
前置詞		文書の目的を問う問題
代名詞		文書の種類〈広告①〉
動詞①〈be 動詞と一般動詞〉		文書の種類〈社内連絡/メモ〉
動詞②〈主述の一致〉		文書の種類〈お知らせ①〉
動詞③〈時制/時〉		文書の種類〈ウェブページ:サービスの申込方法〉
副詞		文書の種類〈求人広告〉
動名詞・不定詞		文書の種類〈E-mail〉
接続詞① 文と文をつなぐ語句		文書の種類 〈複数の文書に関する問題①〉 (解き方のヒント)
接続詞② 前置詞 / 接続詞		文書の種類 〈複数の文書に関する問題②〉 (解き方のヒント)
受動態		文書の種類〈広告②〉
接続詞③ ペアになる語句		文書の種類〈お知らせ②〉

目　次

コア表現リスト　リスニング編　**Listening**

1	I'm calling to ～ / about ～ / because ～	～するために / ～の件で / ～なので 電話をしています
2	Why don't you ～	～してはどうですか
3	I'd like to remind you that ～	再度～をお知らせします
4	I was wondering if you could ～	～していただけませんか
5	I am / We are pleased to announce that ～	～をお知らせすることをうれしく思います
6	I'm having trouble -ing ～	～するのに困っています
7	Please remember to ～	～することを覚えておいてください
8	be available	入手可能です
9	I'm afraid that ～	残念ながら～です
10	We ask that you ～	～していただきますようお願いします
11	You (will) need to ～	～する必要があります
12	I want to let you know that ～	～をお知らせしたいと思います
13	Would you mind -ing ～	～していただけませんか
14	I / We would like to ～	～したいです

コア表現リスト　リーディング編　**Reading**

1	Be sure to ～	必ず～してください
2	I / We suggest that you ～	～することを提案します
3	I am / We are happy to inform you that ～	～をお知らせすることをうれしく思います
4	I / We recommend that you ～	～することを推奨します
5	update ～	～を更新します
6	I am writing to ～ / about ～	～するために / ～の件でお便りしています
7	Please note that ～	～にご注意ください
8	I would appreciate it if you could ～	～していただけるとありがたく思います
9	be required to ～	～することが求められます
10	I / We look forward to ～	～を楽しみにしています
11	I'd like to call / draw your attention to ～	～に注目してください
12	Should 主語＋動詞～ , please ～	万が一～の場合は、～してください
13	be encouraged to ～	～することが推奨されます
14	Please take a moment to ～	お手数ですが、～するようお願いします

No.1 ～ 7　ほぼ確実に設問の正答箇所となる
No.8 ～ 14　非常に高い確率で設問の正答箇所となる

コア表現例文と和訳一覧

Listening

1 I'm calling to ～ / about ～ / because ～

I'm calling to make a restaurant reservation for July 10.

7月10日のレストランの予約をするために電話をしています。

2 Why don't you ～

Why don't you give me a call in two weeks?

2週間後に電話をしていただくのはどうですか。

3 I'd like to remind you that ～

I'd like to remind you that there are only a few seats available for the Tuesday performance.

火曜日の公演には、数席のみ空きがあることを再度お知らせします。

4 I was wondering if you could ～

I was wondering if you could help me with this assignment.

この課題を手伝っていただけませんか。

5 I am / We are pleased to announce that ～

We are pleased to announce that our new products will be on sale this spring.

今春に弊社の新製品が発売されることをお知らせするのをうれしく思います。

6 I'm having trouble -ing ～

I'm having trouble open**ing** this e-mail attachment.

このEメールの添付書類を開けるのに困っています。

7 Please remember to ～

Please remember to change the meeting schedule for next week.

来週の会議の予定を変更することを覚えておいてください。

8 be available
Free food and drinks **are available**.
無料の食事と飲み物が用意されています。

9 I'm afraid that ~
I'm afraid that the flight has been delayed.
申し訳ございませんが、航空便が遅延しています。

10 We ask that you ~
We ask that you use our Web site to contact us.
ご連絡いただくためには弊社のウェブサイトをご利用くださいますようお願いいたします。

11 You (will) need to ~
You need to submit your sales report by the end of this week.
今週末までに売上報告書を提出する必要があります。

12 I want to let you know that ~
I want to let you know that your appointment time has changed.
面会予約の時間が変更したことをお知らせしたいと思います。

13 Would you mind -ing ~
Would you mind help**ing** me look for my mobile phone?
私の携帯電話を探すのを手伝っていただけませんか。

14 I / We would like to ~
I would like to invite you to join our event.
私たちのイベントに参加していただけるようあなたを招待したいと思います。

Reading

1 Be sure to ～

Be sure to download our app by the end of this month.

今月末までに、必ず弊社のアプリをダウンロードしてください。

2 I / We suggest that you ～

I suggest that you visit our Web site to get more information.

さらなる情報を得るために弊社のウェブサイトを訪問することを提案します。

3 I am / We are happy to inform you that ～

We are happy to inform you that our office is moving to a more convenient location.

弊社の事務所が、さらに便利な場所に移転することをお知らせすることをうれしく思います。

4 I / We recommend that you ～

We recommend that you contact the customer service department.

顧客サービス部門に連絡することを推奨します。

5 update ～

We **update** our client list every spring.

弊社は、毎年春に顧客リストを更新します。

6 I am writing to ～ / about ～

I am writing to ask about the delivery of my purchase.

私の購入物の配送に関して尋ねるためにお便りしています。

7 Please note that ～

Please note that the eastern entrance will be closed until next month.

東側の入り口は、来月まで閉鎖されていることにご注意ください。

8 I would appreciate it if you could ～

I would appreciate it if you could schedule a sales meeting in November.

11 月の販売会議の予定を立てていただけるとありがたく思います。

9 be required to ～

All employees **are required to** attend the seminar.

全従業員はセミナーに出席することが要求されます。

10 I / We look forward to ～

We look forward to doing business with you.

御社とお仕事ができることを楽しみにしています。

11 I'd like to call / draw your attention to ～

I'd like to draw your attention to the graphs on the handouts.

配布物のグラフにご注目ください。

12 Should 主語 ＋ 動詞 ～， please ～

Should you have any questions about your order, **please** contact us.

万が一ご注文について質問がある場合は、ご連絡ください。

13 be encouraged to ～

Managers **are encouraged to** contact their volunteers.

責任者がボランティアに連絡することを推奨します。

14 Please take a moment to ～

Please take a moment to fill out the online survey.

お手数ですが、オンラインアンケート調査に記入するようお願いします。

Restaurants

レストラン

Word Bank

次のボキャブラリーの日本語の意味を(　　)内に書き、下のイラストのアルファベットを[　　]内に入れましょう。

① order (　　　　　　　　) [　　　]
② server (　　　　　　　　) [　　　]
③ reservation (　　　　　　　　) [　　　]
④ bill (　　　　　　　　) [　　　]
⑤ menu (　　　　　　　　) [　　　]
⑥ special (　　　　　　　　) [　　　]
⑦ caterer (　　　　　　　　) [　　　]
⑧ appetizer (　　　　　　　　) [　　　]
⑨ buffet (　　　　　　　　) [　　　]
⑩ allergy (　　　　　　　　) [　　　]

Listening Section

Let's Learn!

Part 1 写真描写問題 写真に写っているものに注目―人―

人が主語になるときは、
動詞の現在進行形（be 動詞＋動詞の -ing 形）がよく使われます。

写真に合うものを選びましょう。

1. A server is (taking / eating) an order from a customer.

2. A customer is (sitting / standing) on a chair.

Part 2 応答問題 さまざまな疑問文

Part 2 では最初の発話の多くが疑問文です。

疑問文1-3と応答a-cを読み、正しい応答を選びましょう。

1. Would you like the buffet or today's special? (　　)
2. What's today's special? (　　)
3. Do you have any appetizers? (　　)

a. Yes, of course.
b. Buffet, please.
c. It's roast chicken.

Let's Try!

Part 1 写真描写問題

1-03, 04

それぞれの写真について、４つの説明文のうち適切なものを１つずつ選びましょう。

1.

Ⓐ Ⓑ Ⓒ Ⓓ

2.

Ⓐ Ⓑ Ⓒ Ⓓ

Part 2 応答問題

1-05~09

それぞれの質問の応答として最も適切なものを１つずつ選びましょう。

3. Mark your answer on your answer sheet. Ⓐ Ⓑ Ⓒ

4. Mark your answer on your answer sheet. Ⓐ Ⓑ Ⓒ

5. Mark your answer on your answer sheet. Ⓐ Ⓑ Ⓒ

6. Mark your answer on your answer sheet. Ⓐ Ⓑ Ⓒ

7. Mark your answer on your answer sheet. Ⓐ Ⓑ Ⓒ

Part 3 会話問題

1-10, 11

会話についての設問に対し、最も適切なものを１つずつ選びましょう。

8. Where most likely does the man work?
(A) At a restaurant
(B) At a spa
(C) At a gym
(D) At a bookstore

Ⓐ Ⓑ Ⓒ Ⓓ

9. Why did the woman call?
(A) To invite the man to a party
(B) To cancel a reservation
(C) To reserve a table
(D) To ask about the cost of dinner

Ⓐ Ⓑ Ⓒ Ⓓ

10. What time does the man suggest for dinner?
(A) 8:00 A.M.
(B) 6:00 P.M.
(C) 7:00 P.M.
(D) 8:00 P.M.

Ⓐ Ⓑ Ⓒ Ⓓ

Part 4 説明文問題

1-12, 13

説明文についての設問に対し、最も適切なものを１つずつ選びましょう。

11. Where does the speaker work?
(A) At a grocery store
(B) At a restaurant
(C) At a hamburger shop
(D) At a coffee shop

Ⓐ Ⓑ Ⓒ Ⓓ

12. What is the problem with the menu?
(A) The soup is cold.
(B) The special has changed.
(C) One dish is not available.
(D) It has the wrong prices on it.

Ⓐ Ⓑ Ⓒ Ⓓ

13. What are the listeners asked to do?
(A) Order cream pasta
(B) Wait for the server
(C) Order their food online
(D) Call the server to order

Ⓐ Ⓑ Ⓒ Ⓓ

Reading Section

Let's Learn!

Part 5 短文穴埋め問題　文の構造―主語（S）と述語動詞（V）―

英語の文の多くは、S＋Vで始まります。

（　　　）のうち正しいものを選びましょう。

1. (We update / Update we) our menu every month.
2. (Is our buffet / Our buffet is) available at 7:00 A.M.
3. (Chose Ms. Johnson / Ms. Johnson chose) the shrimp cocktail.
4. (Could you pass / You could pass) me the salt?

Part 6, 7 長文穴埋め問題・読解問題　文書の種類

Part 6と7では、本文の上に文書の種類が書いてあります。

文書の種類の例

a. 記事	**b.** アンケート調査	**c.** 広告
d. Eメール	**e.** 社内連絡 / メモ	**f.** お知らせ

太字の単語に注目して、文書の種類の記号を書きましょう。

1. Questions △△−○○ refer to the following **e-mail**. (　　　)
2. Questions △△−○○ refer to the following **notice**. (　　　)
3. Questions △△−○○ refer to the following **advertisement**. (　　　)
4. Questions △△−○○ refer to the following **memo**. (　　　)
5. Questions △△−○○ refer to the following **survey**. (　　　)
6. Questions △△−○○ refer to the following **article**. (　　　)

Let's Try!

Part 5 短文穴埋め問題

それぞれの空所に入れるのに最も適切なものを1つずつ選びましょう。

14. Be ------- to make your reservation early.
(A) have
(B) take
(C) sure
(D) prior
Ⓐ Ⓑ Ⓒ Ⓓ

15. We would ------- it if you could pay in cash.
(A) appreciate
(B) appreciated
(C) to appreciate
(D) appreciating
Ⓐ Ⓑ Ⓒ Ⓓ

16. Customers with allergies are encouraged ------- talk to their server.
(A) on
(B) to
(C) in
(D) out
Ⓐ Ⓑ Ⓒ Ⓓ

17. Our buffet is available from 7:00 A.M. ------- 10:30 A.M.
(A) with
(B) for
(C) at
(D) through
Ⓐ Ⓑ Ⓒ Ⓓ

18. We update our menu items ------- month.
(A) no
(B) all
(C) one of
(D) every
Ⓐ Ⓑ Ⓒ Ⓓ

19. Ms. Johnson chose the shrimp cocktail for ------- appetizer.
(A) she
(B) her
(C) hers
(D) herself
Ⓐ Ⓑ Ⓒ Ⓓ

Part 6 長文穴埋め問題

それぞれの空所に入れるのに最も適切なものを１つずつ選びましょう。

Questions 20-23 refer to the following advertisement.

Sovay Hotel Restaurant

Enjoy delicious food from around the world at the **Sovay Hotel Restaurant**. We are -------(20.) for breakfast, lunch and dinner. In addition to our regular menu, we -------(21.) daily specials. Hotel guests can pay their restaurant -------(22.) when they pay for their room during check out. Be sure to tell your server that you are a hotel guest before placing your order. --------(23.). You are encouraged to come into the restaurant whenever you are hungry!

20. (A) open
(B) close
(C) closed
(D) opened

Ⓐ Ⓑ Ⓒ Ⓓ

21. (A) have
(B) had
(C) has
(D) having

Ⓐ Ⓑ Ⓒ Ⓓ

22. (A) fares
(B) bills
(C) menus
(D) prices

Ⓐ Ⓑ Ⓒ Ⓓ

23. (A) We give all of the extra food to charity.
(B) Hotel guests can borrow towels.
(C) We only use white napkins.
(D) No reservations are needed.

Ⓐ Ⓑ Ⓒ Ⓓ

Part 7 読解問題

文章を読んで、それぞれの設問の答えとして最も適切なものを1つずつ選びましょう。

Questions 24-26 refer to the following advertisement.

The new Garden Place Restaurant is now open! 

We have delicious food and beautiful gardens. It is a great place for important events or a nice dinner with friends! Dinner starts at 5:00 P.M. each day. Please note that we are very busy in the evening, so call us at 555-2345 to make a reservation!

We are also open for lunch! We have a lunchtime pasta buffet from 11:00 A.M. to 3:00 P.M. every day. Please enjoy all-you-can-eat pasta for only $10 ($12.50 with salad). No reservations are needed. Be sure to tell all of your friends!

24. What is the advertisement for?
(A) A famous restaurant
(B) A new restaurant
(C) A special event
(D) A new dish on the menu

Ⓐ Ⓑ Ⓒ Ⓓ

25. When should customers make reservations?
(A) Customers do not need to make reservations.
(B) When they want to eat lunch
(C) When they want to cook dinner
(D) When they want to eat dinner

Ⓐ Ⓑ Ⓒ Ⓓ

26. What time does the restaurant open for lunch?
(A) 11:00 A.M.
(B) 3:00 P.M.
(C) 5:00 P.M.
(D) 10:00 P.M.

Ⓐ Ⓑ Ⓒ Ⓓ

UNIT 2

Daily Life

日常生活

Word Bank

1-14

次のボキャブラリーの日本語の意味を(　　)内に書き、下のイラストのアルファベットを[　　]内に入れましょう。

① service (　　　　) [　　]
② product (　　　　) [　　]
③ advertisement (　　　　) [　　]
④ survey (　　　　) [　　]
⑤ construction (　　　　) [　　]
⑥ request (　　　　) [　　]
⑦ brochure (　　　　) [　　]
⑧ refrigerator (　　　　) [　　]
⑨ cuisine (　　　　) [　　]
⑩ stove (　　　　) [　　]

Listening Section

Let's Learn!

Part 2 応答問題 疑問詞を使った疑問文

5W（what, who, where, when, which）か 1H（how）で始まる疑問文。How は、how many, how often など、形容詞か副詞とセットになることもあります。

疑問文1-3と応答a-cを読み、正しい応答を選びましょう。

1. Where can I find refrigerators? (　)
2. When does the survey end? (　)
3. How much is the stove? (　)

a. 200 dollars.
b. Saturday.
c. On the third floor.

Part 3 会話問題 設問の特徴

Part 3 で出題される設問は、疑問詞（5W1H）で始まります。

設問1-5が問う内容をa-eから選びましょう。

1. **What** is the conversation mainly about? (　　)
2. **Where** is the conversation taking place? (　　)
3. **Who** is the woman? (　　)
4. **Why** is the man calling? (　　)
5. **How** much does the man pay for the product? (　　)

a. 男性が電話をしている理由
b. 女性の職業
c. 会話のメイントピック
d. 会話が行われている場所
e. 男性が支払う製品の価格

Let's Try!

Part 1 写真描写問題

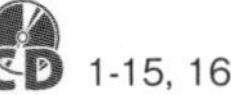

1-15, 16

それぞれの写真について、4つの説明文のうち適切なものを1つずつ選びましょう。

1.

Ⓐ Ⓑ Ⓒ Ⓓ

2.

Ⓐ Ⓑ Ⓒ Ⓓ

Part 2 応答問題

1-17~21

それぞれの質問の応答として最も適切なものを1つずつ選びましょう。

3. Mark your answer on your answer sheet. Ⓐ Ⓑ Ⓒ

4. Mark your answer on your answer sheet. Ⓐ Ⓑ Ⓒ

5. Mark your answer on your answer sheet. Ⓐ Ⓑ Ⓒ

6. Mark your answer on your answer sheet. Ⓐ Ⓑ Ⓒ

7. Mark your answer on your answer sheet. Ⓐ Ⓑ Ⓒ

Part 3 会話問題

1-22, 23

会話についての設問に対し、最も適切なものを１つずつ選びましょう。

8. What is the man's problem?
(A) He can't use his phone.
(B) He doesn't know where to eat.
(C) He doesn't like Italian food.
(D) He can't pay the restaurant.
Ⓐ Ⓑ Ⓒ Ⓓ

9. How did the man first hear about the restaurant?
(A) He saw an advertisement.
(B) The woman told him.
(C) He saw the restaurant.
(D) He has never heard of the restaurant.
Ⓐ Ⓑ Ⓒ Ⓓ

10. What will the man do next?
(A) Write a report
(B) Ask about the cuisine
(C) Call his friend
(D) Make a reservation
Ⓐ Ⓑ Ⓒ Ⓓ

Part 4 説明文問題

1-24, 25

説明文についての設問に対し、最も適切なものを１つずつ選びましょう。

11. Why is the store having a sale?
(A) To celebrate a new store
(B) To return new products
(C) To introduce a new brand
(D) To sell more than another store
Ⓐ Ⓑ Ⓒ Ⓓ

12. Where can customers see a list of featured products?
(A) In a survey
(B) In a brochure
(C) In the newspaper
(D) On an advertisement
Ⓐ Ⓑ Ⓒ Ⓓ

13. Why should customers complete a survey?
(A) To buy a stove
(B) To win a refrigerator
(C) To place an order
(D) To make a reservation
Ⓐ Ⓑ Ⓒ Ⓓ

Reading Section

Let's Learn!

Part 5 短文穴埋め問題　名詞

名詞は、人、もの、ことの名前を表します。
①主語と②目的語は、必ず**名詞**（例文の**太字**）です。
また、(a) 形容詞 (b) 冠詞 (c) 前置詞がある時は、その後ろに**名詞**が来ます。　※形容詞と前置詞の場合は例外あり

My little(a) **sister**① bought a(b) **flower**② at(c) **the shop** yesterday.

(　　　) のうち正しいものを選びましょう。

1. (Advertisements / Advertises) are in the newspaper.
2. Mr. Tanaka will make a (reservation / reserve) soon.
3. The Amazing Restaurant has wonderful (serve / service).
4. Please note that Rockaway Museum is currently under (construct / construction).

Part 7 長文読解問題　文書の種類―アンケート調査(survey)―

アンケート調査とは、商品やサービスに関する質問を客に回答してもらうものです。①～④の項目に注目しましょう。

アンケート調査を見て、下の問題の (　　) のうち正しいものを選びましょう。

① 回答の指示

Congratulations on purchasing a New Cook stove !
Please fill out this survey about your purchase.

② 項目　③ 回答

	Very good	Good	Okay	Poor
Delivery service				✓
Purchase		✓		

④ コメント

Comments: *I like the stove, but I suggest that you put a light on your stoves.*

1. 顧客は、Delivery service（配達サービス）を気に入りましたか。　(はい / いいえ)
2. 顧客は、Purchase（購入品）を気に入りましたか。　(はい / いいえ)
3. Comments（コメント）がありますか。　(はい / いいえ)

Part 5 短文穴埋め問題

それぞれの空所に入れるのに最も適切なものを１つずつ選びましょう。

14. Should you receive the wrong -------, please tell a staff member.
(A) product
(B) production
(C) productivity
(D) produced
Ⓐ Ⓑ Ⓒ Ⓓ

15. I am ------- to ask a question about the advertisement for your product.
(A) write
(B) writing
(C) written
(D) writer
Ⓐ Ⓑ Ⓒ Ⓓ

16. Staff are required to reach ------- targets for each product.
(A) surveys
(B) services
(C) sales
(D) purchases
Ⓐ Ⓑ Ⓒ Ⓓ

17. We are happy to inform you that we will ------- Italian cuisine next month.
(A) offer
(B) offers
(C) offered
(D) offering
Ⓐ Ⓑ Ⓒ Ⓓ

18. Please ------- a moment to read our new product brochure.
(A) open
(B) make
(C) keep
(D) take
Ⓐ Ⓑ Ⓒ Ⓓ

19. Please note that Rockaway Museum is currently ------- construction.
(A) above
(B) on
(C) under
(D) behind
Ⓐ Ⓑ Ⓒ Ⓓ

Part 6 長文穴埋め問題

それぞれの空所に入れるのに最も適切なものを１つずつ選びましょう。

Questions 20-23 refer to the following notice.

Staff Kitchen

Thank you for waiting for us to update the staff kitchen. The construction is now finished! We hope you ------- (20.) like the changes. ------- (21.). In addition, there is a new stove, ------- (22.), and microwave oven. We hope you will enjoy using them. However, we have had a request from the cleaning staff. Please be sure ------- (23.) take all of your food out of the refrigerator every Friday. Should you have any questions, please ask the manager.

20. (A) won't
(B) will
(C) are
(D) were

Ⓐ Ⓑ Ⓒ Ⓓ

21. (A) There is no food allowed.
(B) There are new computers and desks.
(C) There is a new seating area with tables and chairs.
(D) We have kept everything the same.

Ⓐ Ⓑ Ⓒ Ⓓ

22. (A) refrigerator
(B) repeater
(C) reformer
(D) recruiter

Ⓐ Ⓑ Ⓒ Ⓓ

23. (A) in
(B) for
(C) on
(D) to

Ⓐ Ⓑ Ⓒ Ⓓ

Part 7 読解問題

文章を読んで、それぞれの設問の答えとして最も適切なものを１つずつ選びましょう。

Questions 24-26 refer to the following survey.

Congratulations on purchasing a New Cook stove!
Be sure to fill out this survey and register your product.

Name: Alan Monroe
Address: 397 Harrison Court

1. Where did you hear about our products?
☑ a TV advertisement ☐ a radio advertisement ☐ a newspaper advertisement
☐ a Web site ☐ a brochure ☐ other ________

2. What do you think about the delivery service?
☐ 1 Poor ☐ 2 Okay ☐ 3 Good ☑ 4 Very good

3. What do you think about your new stove?
☐ 1 Poor ☐ 2 Okay ☑ 3 Good ☐ 4 Very good

4. Would you recommend a New Cook stove to your friends?
☑ Yes ☐ No

5. We have many other products that might interest you! Please check this box to request a brochure. ☑

Comments:
I like the stove, but it is difficult to see clearly when I am cooking. I suggest that you put a light on your stoves in the future.

24. What is suggested about Mr. Monroe?
(A) He doesn't know how to cook.
(B) He sells stoves.
(C) He never watches television.
(D) He recently bought a new stove.

Ⓐ Ⓑ Ⓒ Ⓓ

25. Where did Mr. Monroe learn about the stove?
(A) A TV advertisement
(B) His friend
(C) A brochure
(D) The Internet

Ⓐ Ⓑ Ⓒ Ⓓ

26. What does Mr. Monroe say about the stove?
(A) He wants it to cook better.
(B) He wants a light.
(C) He wants it to be easier to use.
(D) He thinks it is too heavy.

Ⓐ Ⓑ Ⓒ Ⓓ

Campus Life

学生生活

Word Bank

 1-26

次のボキャブラリーの日本語の意味を(　　)内に書き、下のイラストのアルファベットを[　　]内に入れましょう。

① intern (　　　　　　) [　　　]
② research (　　　　　　) [　　　]
③ course (　　　　　　) [　　　]
④ degree (　　　　　　) [　　　]
⑤ volunteer (　　　　　　) [　　　]
⑥ seminar (　　　　　　) [　　　]
⑦ assignment (　　　　　　) [　　　]
⑧ certificate (　　　　　　) [　　　]
⑨ college (　　　　　　) [　　　]
⑩ campus (　　　　　　) [　　　]

a.

b.

c.

d.

e.

f.

g.

h.

i.

j.

Listening Section

Let's Learn!

Part 1　写真描写問題　写真に写っているものに注目　—もの—

写真に写っているものの位置や人が身につけているものに関する文がよく出題されます。

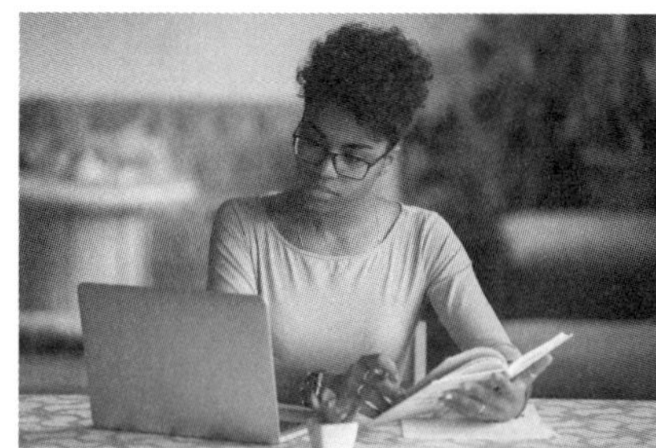

写真に合うものを選びましょう。

1. A (computer / bag) is on the desk.

2. A woman is wearing (a hat / glasses).

Part 4　説明文問題　トークの種類

トークの前の指示文をよく聞きましょう。
ナレーターがトークの種類を言います。

トークの種類の例

a. 広告　　**b.** 電話メッセージ　　**c.** ラジオ放送
d. アナウンス　　**e.** 会議の一部

以下の指示文を読んで、トークの種類の記号を書きましょう。

1. Questions △△ through ○○ refer to the following **announcement**. (　　)
2. Questions △△ through ○○ refer to the following **telephone message**. (　　)
3. Questions △△ through ○○ refer to the following **broadcast**. (　　)
4. Questions △△ through ○○ refer to the following **excerpt from a meeting**. (　　)
5. Questions △△ through ○○ refer to the following **advertisement**. (　　)

Let's Try!

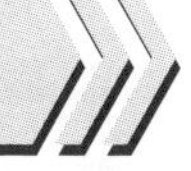

Part 1 写真描写問題

1-27, 28

それぞれの写真について、4つの説明文のうち適切なものを1つずつ選びましょう。

1.

Ⓐ Ⓑ Ⓒ Ⓓ

2.

Ⓐ Ⓑ Ⓒ Ⓓ

Part 2 応答問題

1-29~33

それぞれの質問の応答として最も適切なものを1つずつ選びましょう。

3. Mark your answer on your answer sheet. Ⓐ Ⓑ Ⓒ

4. Mark your answer on your answer sheet. Ⓐ Ⓑ Ⓒ

5. Mark your answer on your answer sheet. Ⓐ Ⓑ Ⓒ

6. Mark your answer on your answer sheet. Ⓐ Ⓑ Ⓒ

7. Mark your answer on your answer sheet. Ⓐ Ⓑ Ⓒ

Part 3 会話問題

会話についての設問に対し、最も適切なものを1つずつ選びましょう。

8. Why is the man visiting the woman?
(A) To sell a product
(B) To turn in an assignment
(C) To do some research
(D) To get advice

Ⓐ Ⓑ Ⓒ Ⓓ

9. What does the woman suggest?
(A) Going to college
(B) Becoming an intern or a volunteer
(C) Getting a full-time job
(D) Starting a research project

Ⓐ Ⓑ Ⓒ Ⓓ

10. What does the man ask the woman to do?
(A) Read a brochure
(B) Complete a survey
(C) Write a letter
(D) Teach a seminar

Ⓐ Ⓑ Ⓒ Ⓓ

Part 4 説明文問題

説明文についての設問に対し、最も適切なものを1つずつ選びましょう。

11. Who most likely are the listeners?
(A) College teachers
(B) New students
(C) Research volunteers
(D) Graduating students

Ⓐ Ⓑ Ⓒ Ⓓ

12. What is the meeting mostly about?
(A) A campus tour
(B) Doing research
(C) Choosing courses
(D) Apartment requests

Ⓐ Ⓑ Ⓒ Ⓓ

13. What does the speaker ask the listeners to do?
(A) Hire an intern
(B) Meet at the buffet
(C) Volunteer to put away the chairs
(D) Bring their course plans to their advisors

Ⓐ Ⓑ Ⓒ Ⓓ

Reading Section

Let's Learn!

Part 5 短文穴埋め問題　形容詞

形容詞（例文では **famous**= 有名な）は、名詞（人、もの、こと）の状態や性質がどのようであるかを表します。
- I have a **famous** friend.　（名詞の前に置かれる）
- My friend is **famous**.　（be 動詞の後ろに置かれる）

（　　　）のうち正しいものを選びましょう。

1. Volunteers are (happy / happiness) to take the course.
2. Please sign up for the (medicine / medical) seminar.
3. All interns need to bring their (recent / recently) certificate.
4. Be sure to finish your last (assign / assignment) by tomorrow.

Part 7 読解問題　文書の種類―テキストメッセージ（text-message chain）―

テキストメッセージとは、スマートフォンやタブレットで 2 人の人が文字を入力して行うやりとりです。①～⑤の項目に注目しましょう。

テキストメッセージを見て、下の問題の（　　）のうち正しいものを選びましょう。

① メッセージを書いた人　② 送信時刻　③ 話題

Jim [1:13 P.M.]	Hi, Mary. Have you finished the assignment for science class yet?
Mary [1:20 P.M.]	Hi, Jim. Not yet. I still need to do some research. We are required to read three papers.
Jim [1:25 P.M.]	I know, but I don't know how to find good papers. ④ 困っていること
Mary [1:27 P.M.]	I can show you how to find them. ⑤ 解決策

1. このテキストメッセージの話題は何ですか。　（学校の宿題 / 会社のコピー機）
2. Mary が最初に返事をしたのはいつですか。　（午後 1 時 13 分 / 午後 1 時 20 分）
3. 困っている Jim を助けるのは誰ですか。　（Mary / 先生）

Let's Try!

Part 5 短文穴埋め問題

それぞれの空所に入れるのに最も適切なものを1つずつ選びましょう。

14. Please note that all ------- interns need to bring their test certificates.
(A) success
(B) succeed
(C) successful
(D) successfully
Ⓐ Ⓑ Ⓒ Ⓓ

15. Volunteers are required to be ------- on Saturday.
(A) spacious
(B) expensive
(C) financial
(D) available
Ⓐ Ⓑ Ⓒ Ⓓ

16. Be sure to finish your ------- by tomorrow.
(A) campus
(B) assignment
(C) volunteer
(D) intern
Ⓐ Ⓑ Ⓒ Ⓓ

17. I ------- that you get a degree in hotel management.
(A) must
(B) suggest
(C) past
(D) biggest
Ⓐ Ⓑ Ⓒ Ⓓ

18. We recommend that you sign up for the seminar ------- soon as possible.
(A) at
(B) so
(C) on
(D) as
Ⓐ Ⓑ Ⓒ Ⓓ

19. Should you have any questions, please ------- the research assistant.
(A) ask
(B) asking
(C) asked
(D) to ask
Ⓐ Ⓑ Ⓒ Ⓓ

Part 6 長文穴埋め問題

それぞれの空所に入れるのに最も適切なものを１つずつ選びましょう。

Questions 20-23 refer to the following letter.

August 15

Grendham University
Office of Admissions
2088 31st St.
Springfield, MA

Dear Ms. Jenkins,

We are happy to inform you that you have been accepted to Grendham University. New students are ------- (20.) to come to ------- (21.) on September 1. On that day, we will explain how to sign up for courses. ------- (22.). You can ask the volunteers questions about college life. Please be sure to arrive ------- (23.) 10:00 A.M. We look forward to seeing you there.

Best regards,

Janice M. Gooding
Registrar

20. (A) require
(B) requires
(C) required
(D) requiring

Ⓐ Ⓑ Ⓒ Ⓓ

21. (A) research
(B) campus
(C) certificate
(D) assignment

Ⓐ Ⓑ Ⓒ Ⓓ

22. (A) Elementary school volunteers will give you a brochure.
(B) Please fill in a survey about the seminar.
(C) To request a special menu, call the caterer.
(D) Student volunteers will lead tours of the campus.

Ⓐ Ⓑ Ⓒ Ⓓ

23. (A) by
(B) after
(C) with
(D) on

Ⓐ Ⓑ Ⓒ Ⓓ

Part 7 読解問題

文章を読んで、それぞれの設問の答えとして最も適切なものを1つずつ選びましょう。

Questions 24-26 refer to the following text message chain.

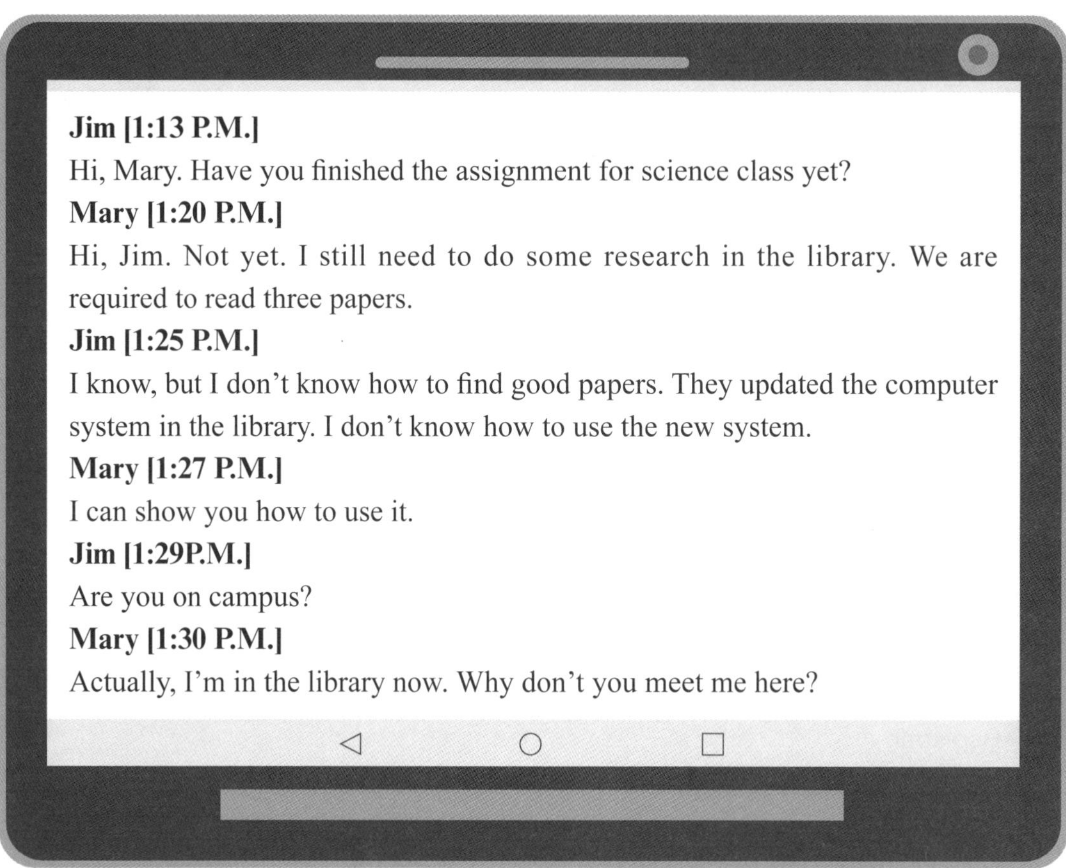

Jim [1:13 P.M.]
Hi, Mary. Have you finished the assignment for science class yet?
Mary [1:20 P.M.]
Hi, Jim. Not yet. I still need to do some research in the library. We are required to read three papers.
Jim [1:25 P.M.]
I know, but I don't know how to find good papers. They updated the computer system in the library. I don't know how to use the new system.
Mary [1:27 P.M.]
I can show you how to use it.
Jim [1:29P.M.]
Are you on campus?
Mary [1:30 P.M.]
Actually, I'm in the library now. Why don't you meet me here?

24. What are Jim and Mary discussing?
(A) The new library building
(B) A big campus event
(C) An assignment for a class
(D) Their computer certificate course

Ⓐ Ⓑ Ⓒ Ⓓ

25. Who is Mary?
(A) A teacher
(B) A classmate of Jim's
(C) A sales intern
(D) A manager

Ⓐ Ⓑ Ⓒ Ⓓ

26. What does Mary offer to do?
(A) Go to Jim's house
(B) Find papers for Jim
(C) Update the computer
(D) Show Jim how to use the new computer system

Ⓐ Ⓑ Ⓒ Ⓓ

Shopping
シヨッピング

Word Bank

1-38

次のボキャブラリーの日本語の意味を(　　)内に書き、下のイラストのアルファベットを[　　]内に入れましょう。

① customer (　　　　) [　　]
② price (　　　　) [　　]
③ discount (　　　　) [　　]
④ payment (　　　　) [　　]
⑤ purchase (　　　　) [　　]
⑥ coupon (　　　　) [　　]
⑦ refund (　　　　) [　　]
⑧ receipt (　　　　) [　　]
⑨ grocery (　　　　) [　　]
⑩ cashier (　　　　) [　　]

Listening Section

Let's Learn!

Part 2 応答問題 Yes/No 疑問文

Do you ～? Is this ～? Can I ～?のように、「(助) 動詞＋主語」で始まる疑問文では、Yes か No で応答が可能です。Sure, I don't think so. や、Yes/No のどちらでもない I'm not sure. のような応答もあります。

疑問文1-3と応答a-cを読み、正しい応答を選びましょう。

1.	Could you do some grocery shopping?	( )	a. Yes, it is.
2.	Are you having trouble using your credit card?	( )	b. No, I'm not.
3.	Is this the discount coupon?	( )	c. Sure, no problem.

Part 3 会話問題 森問題と木問題

設問の中には、会話全体に答えのヒントが散らばっている「森問題」と、会話の一部分に注目する「木問題」があります。

森問題：森全体を見る

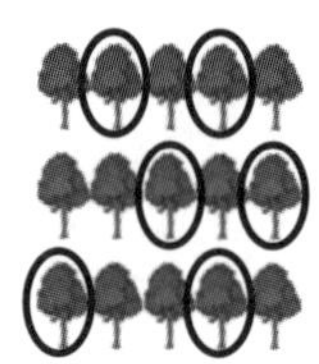

木問題：1 本の木に注目

1. 森問題

このテキストでは、「会話が行われている場所」、「話題」、「話者の職業」など、会話全体の内容がヒントになる設問のことを「森問題」と呼ぶことにします。

2. 木問題

このテキストでは、「問題点」、「理由」、「要望」、「提案」、「行動」など、会話の一部分の内容がヒントになる設問のことを「木問題」と呼ぶことにします。

Let's Try!

Part 1 写真描写問題

 1-39, 40

それぞれの写真について、４つの説明文のうち適切なものを１つずつ選びましょう。

1.

Ⓐ Ⓑ Ⓒ Ⓓ

2.

Ⓐ Ⓑ Ⓒ Ⓓ

Part 2 応答問題

 1-41~45

それぞれの質問の応答として最も適切なものを１つずつ選びましょう。

3. Mark your answer on your answer sheet. Ⓐ Ⓑ Ⓒ

4. Mark your answer on your answer sheet. Ⓐ Ⓑ Ⓒ

5. Mark your answer on your answer sheet. Ⓐ Ⓑ Ⓒ

6. Mark your answer on your answer sheet. Ⓐ Ⓑ Ⓒ

7. Mark your answer on your answer sheet. Ⓐ Ⓑ Ⓒ

Part 3 会話問題

1-46, 47

会話についての設問に対し、最も適切なものを１つずつ選びましょう。

8. Where is the conversation most likely taking place?
(A) A grocery store
(B) A restaurant
(C) An electronics store
(D) A bookstore

Ⓐ Ⓑ Ⓒ Ⓓ

9. What does the woman want to buy?
(A) Cashiers
(B) Coupons
(C) Potatoes
(D) Tomatoes

Ⓐ Ⓑ Ⓒ Ⓓ

10. What will the woman most likely do next?
(A) Buy a book from the man
(B) Ask the cashier for a coupon
(C) Get a brochure about refrigerators
(D) Ask a server for a menu

Ⓐ Ⓑ Ⓒ Ⓓ

Part 4 説明文問題

1-48, 49

説明文についての設問に対し、最も適切なものを１つずつ選びましょう。

11. What is the speaker's problem?
(A) The refrigerator is broken.
(B) Her purchase did not arrive.
(C) She did not pay enough money.
(D) She did not get a discount.

Ⓐ Ⓑ Ⓒ Ⓓ

12. What has the speaker recently done?
(A) Ordered a stove
(B) Gotten a refund
(C) Read a brochure
(D) Bought a refrigerator

Ⓐ Ⓑ Ⓒ Ⓓ

13. What does the speaker ask the listener to do?
(A) Call her
(B) Visit her
(C) Give her a newspaper
(D) Send her an e-mail

Ⓐ Ⓑ Ⓒ Ⓓ

Reading Section

Let's Learn!

Part 5 短文穴埋め問題　前置詞

前置詞とは、at, to, for, from など時や場所を示す語で、名詞や代名詞の前に置かれます。

(　　　) のうち正しいものを選びましょう。

1. We recommend that you call the service center (at / to) 555-3434.
2. Should you have any questions (about / from) our products, please call us.
3. Customers are encouraged to pay (in / for) cash.
4. We look forward to (see / seeing) customers at our new store.

Part 7 読解問題　文書の目的を問う問題

ほとんどの場合、文書の目的は、冒頭部分に書かれていることが多いです。
What is the purpose of the notice?（このお知らせの目的は何ですか。）
Why is the notice written?（なぜこのお知らせは書かれていますか。）

冒頭部分に注目して、お知らせ（notice）の目的を選びましょう。

> To all staff members:
>
> We have updated our refund rules. Please note that customers cannot get a refund for products that they bought during our recent discount sale. Should any customers complain, please tell them to talk to the manager.

文書の目的を問う質問文：What is the purpose of the notice?　(　　)

a. 新しいルールについてスタッフに伝える
b. イベントについてスタッフに知らせる

Let's Try!

Part 5 短文穴埋め問題

それぞれの空所に入れるのに最も適切なものを１つずつ選びましょう。

14. New customers are encouraged to call the service center ------- 555-3434.
(A) for
(B) to
(C) of
(D) at
Ⓐ Ⓑ Ⓒ Ⓓ

15. Please update your address ------- the cashier.
(A) onto
(B) in
(C) toward
(D) with
Ⓐ Ⓑ Ⓒ Ⓓ

16. All employees are ------- to wear an ID badge.
(A) require
(B) requires
(C) required
(D) requiring
Ⓐ Ⓑ Ⓒ Ⓓ

17. ------- you have any questions about your payment, please call us.
(A) Might
(B) Would
(C) Could
(D) Should
Ⓐ Ⓑ Ⓒ Ⓓ

18. We are happy to ------- you that coupons are now available online.
(A) inform
(B) information
(C) informative
(D) informatively
Ⓐ Ⓑ Ⓒ Ⓓ

19. We would like to draw ------- attention to our new grocery section.
(A) you
(B) your
(C) yours
(D) our
Ⓐ Ⓑ Ⓒ Ⓓ

Part 6 長文穴埋め問題

それぞれの空所に入れるのに最も適切なものを１つずつ選びましょう。

Questions 20-23 refer to the following advertisement.

Grady's Grocery

Grady's Grocery is the best grocery store in town! Everyone knows that we sell quality products at great -------(20.). However, this year, we won an award for our great customer service! -------(21.). We are also sending extra coupons to our customer club members. Be sure to look for them in the -------(22.)! We look forward -------(23.) seeing you in our store.

20. (A) purchases
(B) payments
(C) orders
(D) prices

Ⓐ Ⓑ Ⓒ Ⓓ

21. (A) To apologize, we will be giving refunds to all customers.
(B) To improve our service, we will be hiring all new cashiers.
(C) To thank our customers, we will have special discounts all week!
(D) To explain, we are starting a research project.

Ⓐ Ⓑ Ⓒ Ⓓ

22. (A) mail
(B) mails
(C) mailed
(D) mailing

Ⓐ Ⓑ Ⓒ Ⓓ

23. (A) on
(B) at
(C) to
(D) with

Ⓐ Ⓑ Ⓒ Ⓓ

Part 7 読解問題

文章を読んで、それぞれの設問の答えとして最も適切なものを１つずつ選びましょう。

Questions 24-26 refer to the following notice.

Edgerton's Office Supply
4920 Main Street
Fairfax, VA 10293

March 15
To all staff members:

We have updated our refund rules. All customers who would like refunds for their purchases must bring the items and their receipts to the store. Please note that customers cannot get a refund for products that they bought during our recent discount sale. Cashiers cannot give any refunds without checking the price on the receipt. Should any customers complain, please tell them to talk to the manager.

24. What is the purpose of the notice?
(A) To advertise a new service
(B) To tell staff about new rules
(C) To invite the staff to an event
(D) To ask customers for a refund

Ⓐ Ⓑ Ⓒ Ⓓ

25. What do customers need to bring to get a refund?
(A) A brochure
(B) A survey
(C) A bill
(D) A receipt

Ⓐ Ⓑ Ⓒ Ⓓ

26. Who should unhappy customers complain to?
(A) The manager
(B) A cashier
(C) A server
(D) A caterer

Entertainment

エンターテインメント

Word Bank

次のボキャブラリーの日本語の意味を(　　)内に書き、下のイラストのアルファベットを[　　]内に入れましょう。

① event (　　　　　　　　) [　　　]
② museum (　　　　　　　　) [　　　]
③ exhibition (　　　　　　　　) [　　　]
④ vacation (　　　　　　　　) [　　　]
⑤ festival (　　　　　　　　) [　　　]
⑥ theater (　　　　　　　　) [　　　]
⑦ performance (　　　　　　　　) [　　　]
⑧ admission (　　　　　　　　) [　　　]
⑨ audience (　　　　　　　　) [　　　]
⑩ box office (　　　　　　　　) [　　　]

Listening Section

Let's Learn!

Part 1 写真描写問題　写真に写っているものに注目―風景―

人が写っている写真でも「ものの状態や風景」の描写が問われることがあります。

(　　) のうち写真に合うものを選びましょう。

1. The theater doors are (closed / open).

2. The box office is (next to / across from) the doors.

Part 4 説明文問題　トークの種類―ラジオ放送 (broadcast)―

ラジオ放送は放送局と司会者の名前で始まり、メインの話題へとつながります。よく登場する話題には交通情報、天気予報、イベントなどがあります。

ラジオ放送の冒頭部分を見て、下の問題に答えましょう。

放送局と司会者

And now, Channel 5 Community Events. I'm Steve Ronald. We are pleased to announce the annual town festival will be held at Grant Park on July 17…

お知らせ内容

1. 放送局と司会者に下線を引きましょう。
2. お知らせ内容に二重線を引きましょう。

Let's Try!

Part 1 写真描写問題

1-51, 52

それぞれの写真について、4つの説明文のうち適切なものを１つずつ選びましょう。

1.

Ⓐ Ⓑ Ⓒ Ⓓ

2.

Ⓐ Ⓑ Ⓒ Ⓓ

Part 2 応答問題

1-53~57

それぞれの質問の応答として最も適切なものを１つずつ選びましょう。

3. Mark your answer on your answer sheet. Ⓐ Ⓑ Ⓒ

4. Mark your answer on your answer sheet. Ⓐ Ⓑ Ⓒ

5. Mark your answer on your answer sheet. Ⓐ Ⓑ Ⓒ

6. Mark your answer on your answer sheet. Ⓐ Ⓑ Ⓒ

7. Mark your answer on your answer sheet. Ⓐ Ⓑ Ⓒ

Part 3 会話問題

1-58, 59

会話についての設問に対し、最も適切なものを1つずつ選びましょう。

8. Why is the woman calling?
(A) To complain about dinner
(B) To complain about a play
(C) To invite the man to dinner
(D) To invite the man to a play

Ⓐ Ⓑ Ⓒ Ⓓ

9. What does the woman say about "*Grand Mystery*"?
(A) There are no more tickets.
(B) It's very expensive.
(C) It's very popular.
(D) She can't call the box office.

Ⓐ Ⓑ Ⓒ Ⓓ

10. Where will the man and woman meet?
(A) At the theater
(B) In a restaurant
(C) At the office
(D) In a café

Ⓐ Ⓑ Ⓒ Ⓓ

Part 4 説明文問題

1-60, 61

説明文についての設問に対し、最も適切なものを1つずつ選びましょう。

11. What is happening in July?
(A) A sports event
(B) A music contest
(C) The town festival
(D) The grand opening of a restaurant

Ⓐ Ⓑ Ⓒ Ⓓ

12. How much does it cost to go to the festival?
(A) One dollar
(B) Five dollars
(C) Ten dollars
(D) Nothing

Ⓐ Ⓑ Ⓒ Ⓓ

13. What does the speaker remind people to do?
(A) Bring water
(B) Eat food
(C) Take a survey
(D) Visit a museum

Ⓐ Ⓑ Ⓒ Ⓓ

Reading Section

Let's Learn!

Part 5 短文穴埋め問題 代名詞

代名詞は名詞の代わりに使われ、(1)主格(2)所有格(3)目的格(4)所有代名詞(5)再帰代名詞があります。

I like **my** English teacher. How is **yours**?
(1) (2) (4)

I like **her** because **she** is clever. **She** taught **herself** Chinese.
(3) (1) (1) (5)

下の代名詞の表を完成させましょう。

	主格 〜は (主語になる)	所有格 〜の(後ろに名詞がくる)	目的格 〜を・〜に(動詞や前置詞の目的語になる)	所有代名詞 〜のもの	再帰代名詞 〜自身
私	I	my	me	mine	myself
あなた	you	②( )	you	yours	yourself
彼	he	his	him	his	⑤( )
彼女	she	her	③( )	hers	herself
それ	it	its	it	-	itself
私たち	we	our	us	④( )	ourselves
あなたたち	you	your	you	yours	yourselves
彼(女)ら・それら	①( )	their	them	theirs	themselves

上の表の( )に入る代名詞を、以下の同じ番号の文の( )に書きましょう。

① ( ) are my friends.
② Can I ask ( ) name?
③ I talked to ( ) yesterday.
④ Your school is older than ( ).
⑤ Tom bought a new car for ( ).

Part 7 読解問題 文書の種類—広告①(advertisement)—

広告では、商品、サービス、イベント、セール、店のオープンなどを宣伝します。①〜③の項目に注目しましょう。

広告を見て、下の問題の( )のうち正しいものを選びましょう。

① イベントの種類

The Hampton Museum is pleased to announce that it will be hosting a special exhibition of paintings by Mulligan. The exhibition will be from October 1 to October 31. We recommend that you get your tickets early because the exhibition will be very popular.

② 詳細

③ 指示内容

1. 何の広告ですか。(展示会 / セール)
2. このイベントの開催期間はどれくらいですか。(1ヶ月 / 3ヶ月)
3. 読み手は何をすべきですか。(早めにチケットを購入する / クーポンを利用する)

Let's Try!

Part 5 短文穴埋め問題

それぞれの空所に入れるのに最も適切なものを１つずつ選びましょう。

14. Be sure to pay for ------- theater tickets by June 30.
(A) you
(B) your
(C) yours
(D) yourself
Ⓐ Ⓑ Ⓒ Ⓓ

15. The Granger Gallery will update ------- exhibition calendar next week.
(A) them
(B) it
(C) its
(D) it's
Ⓐ Ⓑ Ⓒ Ⓓ

16. All audience members are required ------- turn off their phones during the performance.
(A) of
(B) for
(C) in
(D) to
Ⓐ Ⓑ Ⓒ Ⓓ

17. We look forward to ------- the event next week.
(A) attended
(B) attend
(C) attending
(D) to attend
Ⓐ Ⓑ Ⓒ Ⓓ

18. Please note that the museum is open ------- weekdays.
(A) on
(B) in
(C) for
(D) at
Ⓐ Ⓑ Ⓒ Ⓓ

19. We are happy to inform you that discount tickets are ------- at the box office.
(A) possible
(B) available
(C) responsible
(D) fashionable
Ⓐ Ⓑ Ⓒ Ⓓ

Part 6 長文穴埋め問題

それぞれの空所に入れるのに最も適切なものを1つずつ選びましょう。

Questions 20-23 refer to the following advertisement.

The Ground Hall Players

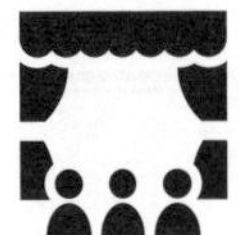

Do you want to do something interesting this summer -------(20.)? Do you like the theater? -------(21.). This summer, we will do eight performances of a new play called "*The Duck and the Drum*". Don't -------(22.) your chance to act in front of a live audience! Be sure -------(23.) sign up today at the Ground Hall Theater box office.

20. (A) job
(B) vacation
(C) dress
(D) storm

Ⓐ Ⓑ Ⓒ Ⓓ

21. (A) Then, please take a moment to buy a refrigerator.
(B) In that case, we look forward to eating at the buffet.
(C) If not, we recommend that you watch a play.
(D) If so, we encourage you to join our performance group!

Ⓐ Ⓑ Ⓒ Ⓓ

22. (A) miss
(B) missed
(C) missing
(D) to miss

Ⓐ Ⓑ Ⓒ Ⓓ

23. (A) for
(B) at
(C) of
(D) to

Ⓐ Ⓑ Ⓒ Ⓓ

Part 7 読解問題

文章を読んで、それぞれの設問の答えとして最も適切なものを１つずつ選びましょう。

Questions 24-26 refer to the following advertisement.

The Hampton Museum is pleased to announce that it will be hosting a special exhibition of paintings by Mulligan. The exhibition will be from October 1 to October 31. We recommend that you get your tickets early because the exhibition will be very popular. Admission is $10 for adults and $5 for children. Please note that the museum will be closed for construction from November 1 to December 31, so enjoy the paintings while you can!

24. What type of event will be held at the Hampton Museum in October?
(A) An art exhibition
(B) A music concert
(C) A theater performance
(D) A movie festival

Ⓐ Ⓑ Ⓒ Ⓓ

25. How much must an adult pay to see the paintings?
(A) $5
(B) $10
(C) $25
(D) $31

Ⓐ Ⓑ Ⓒ Ⓓ

26. What will happen in November?
(A) There will be free admission.
(B) The performance will start.
(C) The museum will be closed.
(D) The museum will open.

Ⓐ Ⓑ Ⓒ Ⓓ

Office Work (1)

オフィスの仕事 (1)

Word Bank

次のボキャブラリーの日本語の意味を(　　)内に書き、下のイラストのアルファベットを[　　]内に入れましょう。

① company (　　　　　　) [　　　]
② president (　　　　　　) [　　　]
③ colleague (　　　　　　) [　　　]
④ supervisor (　　　　　　) [　　　]
⑤ representative (　　　　　　) [　　　]
⑥ branch (　　　　　　) [　　　]
⑦ cabinet (　　　　　　) [　　　]
⑧ headquarters (　　　　　　) [　　　]
⑨ manager (　　　　　　) [　　　]
⑩ shelf (　　　　　　) [　　　]

Listening Section

Let's Learn!

Part 2 応答問題　選択疑問文

orを使って「Aですか、またはBですか」と選択を促す疑問文です。
例：Do you need the report now or later?
Are you leaving in the morning or in the afternoon?

以下の質問の応答として、それぞれの場合に合うものを選びましょう。
質問：Would you like to go out for a movie or dinner?

- どちらかを選ぶ　(Movie. / Both. / Neither. / Either.)
- 両方選ぶ　(Movie. / Both. / Neither. / Either.)
- どちらも選ばない　(Movie. / Both. / Neither. / Either.)
- どちらでもよい　(Movie. / Both. / Neither. / Either.)

Part 3 会話問題　森問題―話題―

話題を問う設題は森問題です。会話全体に答えのヒントが散らばっています。
What is the conversation mainly about?（この会話は主に何についてですか。）
What are the speakers discussing?（話し手は何について話していますか。）
などの質問で問われます。

以下の会話文は、話題を問う問題のヒントのみを残し、それ以外の単語を消しています。

M: ________ the manager ________ leaving ________.
________________ the new manager?
W: ____ nice ____ new challenge. ____________?
M: __________! ____________.
W: ________ I will. ____ ask about the job ____.
M: ______________. ____________.

話題を問う質問文：What is the conversation mainly about?　(　　)
これを見て、下の問題のa-cのうち正しいものを選びましょう。

a. マネージャーになること
b. 改装工事が行われること
c. 新しい棚を購入すること

Let's Try!

Part 1 写真描写問題

1-63, 64

それぞれの写真について、4つの説明文のうち適切なものを１つずつ選びましょう。

1.

Ⓐ Ⓑ Ⓒ Ⓓ

2.

Ⓐ Ⓑ Ⓒ Ⓓ

Part 2 応答問題

1-65~69

それぞれの質問の応答として最も適切なものを１つずつ選びましょう。

3. Mark your answer on your answer sheet. Ⓐ Ⓑ Ⓒ

4. Mark your answer on your answer sheet. Ⓐ Ⓑ Ⓒ

5. Mark your answer on your answer sheet. Ⓐ Ⓑ Ⓒ

6. Mark your answer on your answer sheet. Ⓐ Ⓑ Ⓒ

7. Mark your answer on your answer sheet. Ⓐ Ⓑ Ⓒ

Part 3 会話問題

1-70, 71

会話についての設問に対し、最も適切なものを１つずつ選びましょう。

8. What are the speakers discussing?
(A) Moving to a new office
(B) Becoming a manager
(C) Working at a different company
(D) Buying a new cabinet
Ⓐ Ⓑ Ⓒ Ⓓ

9. When does the woman say she will ask about the job?
(A) Today
(B) Tomorrow
(C) Next week
(D) Next month
Ⓐ Ⓑ Ⓒ Ⓓ

10. What does the man say the woman should do?
(A) Send an e-mail message
(B) Go to the headquarters building
(C) Call the company president
(D) Talk to the headquarters staff
Ⓐ Ⓑ Ⓒ Ⓓ

Part 4 説明文問題

1-72, 73

説明文についての設問に対し、最も適切なものを１つずつ選びましょう。

11. What is the purpose of the advertisement?
(A) To find new workers
(B) To explain a problem
(C) To sell office furniture
(D) To announce a new store opening
Ⓐ Ⓑ Ⓒ Ⓓ

12. What is happening this month?
(A) Some items are on sale.
(B) The store will be closed.
(C) A new store will open.
(D) New products will be available.
Ⓐ Ⓑ Ⓒ Ⓓ

13. How can customers get a brochure?
(A) Purchase some furniture
(B) Ask the manager
(C) Check the Web site
(D) Call the company
Ⓐ Ⓑ Ⓒ Ⓓ

Reading Section

Let's Learn!

Part 5 短文穴埋め問題 動詞①―be 動詞と一般動詞―

動詞は大きく分けて 2 種類あります。

1. be 動詞（is, am, are, was, were）: be 動詞は主語と後ろの語句をつなぐ「＝（イコール）」の働きがあります。
2. 一般動詞：動作（come, go, etc.）、気持ち（like, think, etc.）などを表します。

（　　　）のうち正しいものを選びましょう。

1. Ms. Stone (likes / is) her new office.
2. They (go / are) my coworkers.
3. We (updated / were) the manager's contact information.
4. I (am / received) new cabinets today.

Part 7 読解問題 文書の種類―社内連絡 / メモ (memo)―

社内連絡 / メモは社員へ向けた連絡事項です。
社内イベントや新規採用者に関するお知らせがよく出題されます。

社内連絡を見て、下の問題の（ ）のうち正しいものを選びましょう。

To: All staff
From: Personnel Department
Subject: Intern program

We are pleased to announce that Manitor Company will be starting a new intern program this summer. University business students will be encouraged to apply. Interns will work with a supervisor at one of our branches. Please note that interested students should be sure to apply before May 15.

① 話題　② 詳細　③ 注意事項

1. この社内連絡の話題は何ですか。　（夏のプログラム / 秋のプログラム）
2. このプログラムの対象者は誰ですか。　（学生 / 顧客）
3. 何に注意すればよいですか。　（申込期日がある / 人数制限がある）

Let's Try!

Part 5 短文穴埋め問題

それぞれの空所に入れるのに最も適切なものを１つずつ選びましょう。

14. We ------- the manager's contact information last week.
(A) update
(B) updated
(C) updates
(D) updating
Ⓐ Ⓑ Ⓒ Ⓓ

15. We suggest that you ------- using plastic bags.
(A) stop
(B) stops
(C) stopped
(D) stopping
Ⓐ Ⓑ Ⓒ Ⓓ

16. We ------- happy to inform you that Mr. Smith will be our new branch manager.
(A) is
(B) am
(C) are
(D) was
Ⓐ Ⓑ Ⓒ Ⓓ

17. Sales representatives are encouraged to fill ------- the survey.
(A) over
(B) on
(C) out
(D) with
Ⓐ Ⓑ Ⓒ Ⓓ

18. I'd like to ------- your attention to the brochures on the shelves.
(A) dry
(B) drink
(C) drive
(D) draw
Ⓐ Ⓑ Ⓒ Ⓓ

19. New cabinets will be ------- before the president visits.
(A) delivering
(B) delivered
(C) delivery
(D) deliver
Ⓐ Ⓑ Ⓒ Ⓓ

Part 6 長文穴埋め問題

それぞれの空所に入れるのに最も適切なものを１つずつ選びましょう。

Questions 20-23 refer to the following memo.

From: Grant Jones
To: Sales Staff
Date: September 16
Re: Sales Planning Meeting

I am writing to remind you that our sales meeting will be ------- (**20.**) September 23 at the company headquarters. Two representatives from each ------- (**21.**) will attend the meeting. ------- (**22.**). Should you have any questions, please ------- (**23.**) the sales team manager.

20. (A) by
(B) in
(C) at
(D) on

Ⓐ Ⓑ Ⓒ Ⓓ

21. (A) audience
(B) headquarters
(C) branch
(D) course

Ⓐ Ⓑ Ⓒ Ⓓ

22. (A) We really enjoyed the speaker's talk.
(B) Be sure to bring the sales reports for your branch.
(C) We recommend that you buy your tickets early.
(D) Please note that the new cabinet will arrive on Thursday.

Ⓐ Ⓑ Ⓒ Ⓓ

23. (A) contact
(B) contacts
(C) contacted
(D) contacting

Ⓐ Ⓑ Ⓒ Ⓓ

Part 7 読解問題

文章を読んで、それぞれの設問の答えとして最も適切なものを１つずつ選びましょう。

Questions 24-26 refer to the following memo.

MEMO

From: Human Resources Department
To: All employees
Re: Summer internship program

We are pleased to announce that Manitor Company will be starting a new intern program this summer. University business students will be encouraged to apply. Interns will work with a supervisor at one of our branches. Interns will also attend a weekly seminar led by one of our managers. Interns will be required to work five days per week from August 1 to September 10. Please note that interested students should be sure to apply before May 15.

24. What is the purpose of the memo?
(A) To explain a rule
(B) To advertise a new product
(C) To introduce a new company
(D) To announce a summer intern program

Ⓐ Ⓑ Ⓒ Ⓓ

25. Who should apply to be an intern?
(A) Science students
(B) Business students
(C) Art students
(D) Computer students

Ⓐ Ⓑ Ⓒ Ⓓ

26. How many days must interns work each week?
(A) Three
(B) Four
(C) Five
(D) Six

Ⓐ Ⓑ Ⓒ Ⓓ

Office Work (2)

オフィスの仕事 (2)

Word Bank

次のボキャブラリーの日本語の意味を(　　)内に書き、下のイラストのアルファベットを[　　]内に入れましょう。

① conference (　　　　) [　　]
② client (　　　　) [　　]
③ equipment (　　　　) [　　]
④ contract (　　　　) [　　]
⑤ budget (　　　　) [　　]
⑥ workshop (　　　　) [　　]
⑦ document (　　　　) [　　]
⑧ deadline (　　　　) [　　]
⑨ shipment (　　　　) [　　]
⑩ inventory (　　　　) [　　]

Listening Section

Let's Learn!

Part 1　写真描写問題　位置を表す語（句）

Part 1 ではものの位置を表す語（句）がよく登場します。
例えば on（～の上に）、in front of（～の前に）、next to（～のとなりに）などがあります。

(　　) のうち写真に合うものを選びましょう。

1. There are some chairs (next to each other / above the table).

2. A TV screen is (on / under) the wall.

Part 4　説明文問題　トークの種類　―会議の一部①(excerpt from a meeting)―

会議の一部は、社員への連絡事項やビジネス関連の話題が取り上げられます。

会議の一部を見て、以下の問題に答えましょう。

① 話題

Okay, everyone, now let's talk about shipments. We are sending a big shipment for a client. It will take more than three hours to prepare. I'd like to remind you that the deadline is 10 A.M. tomorrow.

② 詳細

③注意 / 指示内容

1. 会議の話題に下線を引きましょう。

2. 注意事項に下線を引きましょう。

Let's Try!

Part 1 写真描写問題

1-75, 76

それぞれの写真について、4つの説明文のうち適切なものを１つずつ選びましょう。

1.

Ⓐ Ⓑ Ⓒ Ⓓ

2.

Ⓐ Ⓑ Ⓒ Ⓓ

Part 2 応答問題

1-77~81

それぞれの質問の応答として最も適切なものを１つずつ選びましょう。

3. Mark your answer on your answer sheet. Ⓐ Ⓑ Ⓒ

4. Mark your answer on your answer sheet. Ⓐ Ⓑ Ⓒ

5. Mark your answer on your answer sheet. Ⓐ Ⓑ Ⓒ

6. Mark your answer on your answer sheet. Ⓐ Ⓑ Ⓒ

7. Mark your answer on your answer sheet. Ⓐ Ⓑ Ⓒ

Part 3 会話問題

会話についての設問に対し、最も適切なものを１つずつ選びましょう。

8. Who is the man?
(A) A customer
(B) A cashier
(C) The woman's client
(D) The woman's colleague

Ⓐ Ⓑ Ⓒ Ⓓ

9. What must the woman finish by this afternoon?
(A) A presentation
(B) A contract
(C) A workshop
(D) A shipment

Ⓐ Ⓑ Ⓒ Ⓓ

10. What does the woman ask the man to do?
(A) Buy some equipment
(B) Make a presentation
(C) E-mail budget information
(D) Give her a refund

Ⓐ Ⓑ Ⓒ Ⓓ

Part 4 説明文問題

説明文についての設問に対し、最も適切なものを１つずつ選びましょう。

11. What is the speaker mainly talking about?
(A) Meeting the president
(B) Preparing a shipment
(C) Making a purchase
(D) Calling a caterer

Ⓐ Ⓑ Ⓒ Ⓓ

12. Who most likely are the listeners?
(A) A group of colleagues
(B) Company clients
(C) The speaker's managers
(D) New caterers

Ⓐ Ⓑ Ⓒ Ⓓ

13. When must the task be finished?
(A) 7:00 A.M.
(B) 10:00 A.M.
(C) 10:00 P.M.
(D) 12:00 P.M.

Ⓐ Ⓑ Ⓒ Ⓓ

Reading Section

Let's Learn!

Part 5 短文穴埋め問題　動詞②—主述の一致—

英語では、主語が単数か複数かによって述語動詞の形が変わります。ただし、規則変化をしない動詞もあるので注意しましょう。
- be 動詞：主語が 3 人称単数の時は is/was、複数の時は are/were
- 一般動詞：主語が 3 人称単数で、時制が現在の時は述語動詞の語尾に -s がつきます。

（　　　）のうち正しいものを選びましょう。

1. Mr. Tanaka (knows / know) about next year's budget.
2. We (look / looks) forward to interviewing Mr. Smith this afternoon.
3. All the cabinets in the office (are / is) broken.
4. Rocky Rally Inc. (has / have) just updated its homepage.

Part 7 読解問題　文書の種類 —お知らせ①（notice / announcement）—

お知らせでは、主に告知、案内、警告、注意などが伝えられます。
①〜③の項目に注目しましょう。

お知らせを見て、下の問題の（　　　）のうち正しいものを選びましょう。

International Hotel Association Conference
Tacoma, Washington
February 9-12

We are pleased to announce the new International Hotel Association Conference! There will be exciting workshops and exhibitions each day. Be sure to register for the conference before the deadline on December 10. We look forward to seeing you in Washington!

②詳細

③指示内容

1. このお知らせの話題は何ですか。　（会議 / 改装工事）
2. どんな催し物がありますか。　（ワークショップ / 食事会）
3. 読み手は何をすべきですか。　（期日までに申し込む / 発表の準備をする）

Let's Try!

Part 5 短文穴埋め問題

それぞれの空所に入れるのに最も適切なものを１つずつ選びましょう。

14. We look forward to ------- Mr. Smith this afternoon.
(A) see
(B) seen
(C) saw
(D) seeing
Ⓐ Ⓑ Ⓒ Ⓓ

15. The client ------- this morning about the budget proposal.
(A) call
(B) called
(C) calling
(D) have called
Ⓐ Ⓑ Ⓒ Ⓓ

16. We are happy to ------- you that Ms. Skogs will join the budget team.
(A) inform
(B) information
(C) informative
(D) informed
Ⓐ Ⓑ Ⓒ Ⓓ

17. I'm writing to tell you that the shipment of kitchen ------- was delayed.
(A) equipment
(B) document
(C) apartment
(D) comment
Ⓐ Ⓑ Ⓒ Ⓓ

18. Be sure to sign up for the next workshop ------- the September 10th deadline.
(A) after
(B) for
(C) at
(D) by
Ⓐ Ⓑ Ⓒ Ⓓ

19. You are ------- to submit the document by the end of this month.
(A) replied
(B) acquired
(C) required
(D) responded
Ⓐ Ⓑ Ⓒ Ⓓ

Part 6 長文穴埋め問題

それぞれの空所に入れるのに最も適切なものを1つずつ選びましょう。

Questions 20-23 refer to the following memo.

From: Jeremy Frasier
To: All managers and supervisors
Date: January 23
Re: Training workshop

All supervisors are required to attend a ------- (20.) next week. During the workshop, we will explain the new inventory tracking equipment. We will also discuss ideas ------- (21.) preparing shipments more quickly. ------- (22.). They will be on Monday morning and Tuesday afternoon. Staff can choose which workshop to attend. I suggest ------- (23.) you sign up for your preferred time as soon as possible.

20. (A) buffet
(B) performance
(C) workshop
(D) exhibition

Ⓐ Ⓑ Ⓒ Ⓓ

21. (A) for
(B) to
(C) on
(D) in

Ⓐ Ⓑ Ⓒ Ⓓ

22. (A) I would appreciate it if you could put the coupons in the cabinet.
(B) Be sure to make your purchase before the meeting.
(C) You can use the stove to make any type of cuisine.
(D) Please note that the same workshop will be held two times.

Ⓐ Ⓑ Ⓒ Ⓓ

23. (A) it
(B) that
(C) if
(D) on

Ⓐ Ⓑ Ⓒ Ⓓ

Part 7 読解問題

文章を読んで、それぞれの設問の答えとして最も適切なものを１つずつ選びましょう。

Questions 24-26 refer to the following notice.

International Hotel Association Conference

Tacoma, Washington
February 9-12

We are pleased to announce the new International Hotel Association Conference! There will be different workshops each day. There are many exciting topics, such as better advertising, improving customer service, and new reservation technology. In addition, we encourage you to visit our exhibition hall, where representatives from more than 100 companies will show the latest hotel products and equipment. There will be useful products for every budget. Be sure to register for the conference before the deadline on December 10. We look forward to seeing you in Washington!

24. For whom is the notice most likely intended?
(A) Managers of factories
(B) Volunteers in schools
(C) Workers in hotels
(D) Presidents of banks

Ⓐ Ⓑ Ⓒ Ⓓ

25. What is indicated about the workshops?
(A) There are many topics each day.
(B) They have been canceled.
(C) They cost extra money.
(D) People can only attend one.

Ⓐ Ⓑ Ⓒ Ⓓ

26. What will be in the exhibition hall?
(A) A construction project
(B) More than 100 paintings
(C) A certificate course
(D) Displays of products and equipment

Bank & Post office

銀行&郵便局

Word Bank

1-86

次のボキャブラリーの日本語の意味を(　　)内に書き、下のイラストのアルファベットを[　　]内に入れましょう。

① delivery ( ) [ ]
② account ( ) [ ]
③ package ( ) [ ]
④ identification ( ) [ ]
⑤ credit card ( ) [ ]
⑥ deposit ( ) [ ]
⑦ signature ( ) [ ]
⑧ balance ( ) [ ]
⑨ envelope ( ) [ ]
⑩ form ( ) [ ]

a.

b.
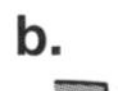

c.

d.
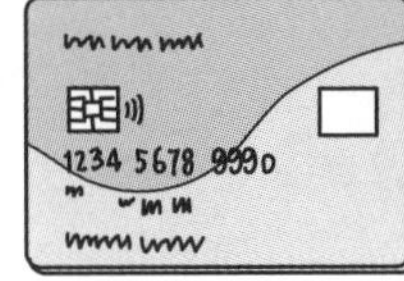

e.

f.

g.

h.

i.

j.

Listening Section

Let's Learn!

Part 2 応答問題　付加疑問文

「〜ですね」と相手に同意を求めたり、「〜ですよね」と念を押したりするときに使います。The event is tomorrow, isn't it? のように、文の最後に isn't it? don't you? などを付け足して疑問文にします。

疑問文1-3と応答a-cを読み、正しい応答を選びましょう。

1. This is your signature, isn't it? 　(　) a. Certainly, sir.
2. You accept credit cards, don't you? 　(　) b. No, that's Mr. Kelly's.
3. I don't need to show my identification, do I? (　) c. Actually, you do.

Part 3 会話問題　森問題—職業—

職業を問う問題は森問題です。会話全体に答えのヒントが散らばっています。Who is the man?（男性は誰ですか）や What most likely is the woman's job?（女性の職業は何だと考えられますか）などの質問で問われます。

下の会話文は、職業を問う問題のヒントのある箇所のみを残し、それ以外の単語を消しています。

W: ____________, I would like to mail a book.
M: ____________. __________________?
W: __________________.
M: ____________, why don't you use one of our special envelopes? It will be cheaper than a package.

職業を問う質問文：Who is the man?　(　　)
これを見て、下の問題のa-cのうち正しいものを選びましょう。

a. 図書館の職員
b. 銀行員
c. 郵便局員

Let's Try!

Part 1 写真描写問題

 1-87, 88

それぞれの写真について、4つの説明文のうち適切なものを1つずつ選びましょう。

1.

Ⓐ Ⓑ Ⓒ Ⓓ

2.

Ⓐ Ⓑ Ⓒ Ⓓ

Part 2 応答問題

 1-89~93

それぞれの質問の応答として最も適切なものを1つずつ選びましょう。

3. Mark your answer on your answer sheet. Ⓐ Ⓑ Ⓒ

4. Mark your answer on your answer sheet. Ⓐ Ⓑ Ⓒ

5. Mark your answer on your answer sheet. Ⓐ Ⓑ Ⓒ

6. Mark your answer on your answer sheet. Ⓐ Ⓑ Ⓒ

7. Mark your answer on your answer sheet. Ⓐ Ⓑ Ⓒ

Part 3 会話問題

1-94, 95

会話についての設問に対し、最も適切なものを１つずつ選びましょう。

8. Who is the man?
(A) A bank teller
(B) A library clerk
(C) A post office worker
(D) A server

Ⓐ Ⓑ Ⓒ Ⓓ

9. What does the man suggest?
(A) Using a special envelope
(B) Sending a package
(C) Buying a book
(D) Opening an account

Ⓐ Ⓑ Ⓒ Ⓓ

10. What will the woman probably do next?
(A) Pay with cash
(B) Pay with a credit card
(C) Check her account balance
(D) Send a package

Ⓐ Ⓑ Ⓒ Ⓓ

Part 4 説明文問題

1-96, 97

説明文についての設問に対し、最も適切なものを１つずつ選びましょう。

11. Who most likely is the speaker?
(A) An event caterer
(B) A store customer
(C) A box office manager
(D) A bank representative

Ⓐ Ⓑ Ⓒ Ⓓ

12. What is the problem with Ms. Smith's deposit?
(A) It was too large.
(B) It was too late.
(C) She did not sign the form.
(D) She did not write her account number.

Ⓐ Ⓑ Ⓒ Ⓓ

13. What does the speaker ask Ms. Smith to do?
(A) Use a credit card
(B) Come to the bank
(C) Talk to the supervisor
(D) Get a refund

Ⓐ Ⓑ Ⓒ Ⓓ

Reading Section

Let's Learn!

Part 5 短文穴埋め問題　動詞③―時制／時―

いつのこと（過去、現在、未来）を表しているかは、動詞の活用または、文中の時を表すキーワードを見るとわかります。キーワードから、適切な述語動詞を選びましょう。
過去：yesterday, ago など；現在：every day, always など；
未来：tomorrow, later など

（　　　）のうち正しいものを選びましょう。

1. I (check / checked) my account balance yesterday.
2. The delivery date (changed / will change) three days ago.
3. Customers (will be / were) able to make deposits tomorrow.
4. Most of our employees carry their identification cards (every day / last year).

Part 7 読解問題　文書の種類―ウェブページ(Web page)：サービスの申込方法―

ウェブページの問題では、イベントやサービスの説明など、さまざまな内容が扱われます。①〜③の項目に注目しましょう。

ウェブページの一部を見て、下の問題の（　　）のうち正しいものを選びましょう。

United Bank Online
<u>How to open a new account</u>　① 話題
It's easy! Just follow these four simple steps:
1. Prepare two types of identification documents.　② 詳細
2. Bring the documents and your deposit to the bank.
3. Complete the new account form.
4. Wait a few minutes for the staff to give you a bank card.　③ 読み手へのメッセージ
We look forward to seeing you at one of our branches soon.

1. このウェブページの話題は何ですか。　(銀行口座の開き方 / 小包の送り方)
2. 1 から 4 の数字は何を表していますか。　(読み手が行うこと / 郵便物の種類)
3. 読み手へのメッセージはどんなものですか。　(警告 / 勧誘)

Let's Try!

Part 5 短文穴埋め問題

それぞれの空所に入れるのに最も適切なものを１つずつ選びましょう。

14. Please note that the delivery time ------- last week.
(A) change
(B) changed
(C) changes
(D) will change
Ⓐ Ⓑ Ⓒ Ⓓ

15. We are happy to inform you that customers ------- able to make deposits tomorrow.
(A) were
(B) have been
(C) had been
(D) will be
Ⓐ Ⓑ Ⓒ Ⓓ

16. Employees are required to carry ------- identification cards at all times.
(A) your
(B) their
(C) his
(D) my
Ⓐ Ⓑ Ⓒ Ⓓ

17. Be sure to check your ------- balance regularly.
(A) account
(B) signature
(C) package
(D) delivery
Ⓐ Ⓑ Ⓒ Ⓓ

18. ------- you need more envelopes, please ask your manager.
(A) Must
(B) Might
(C) Should
(D) Could
Ⓐ Ⓑ Ⓒ Ⓓ

19. I would appreciate it if you could put this deposit ------- the account for me.
(A) behind
(B) for
(C) onto
(D) in
Ⓐ Ⓑ Ⓒ Ⓓ

Part 6 長文穴埋め問題

それぞれの空所に入れるのに最も適切なものを１つずつ選びましょう。

Questions 20-23 refer to the following e-mail.

To: Miranda Hartley
From: Abel's Electronics
Subject: Updated Delivery Date

Ms. Hartley,

We are happy to inform you that we were able -------(20.) your package early. The new -------(21.) date is April 12. Please note that we need your signature on a form when the package is delivered. -------(22.). If you are not available -------(23.) April 12, be sure to schedule a different delivery time on our Web site.

Best regards,

The Abel's Electronics Team

20. (A) will send
(B) sending
(C) sent
(D) to send

Ⓐ Ⓑ Ⓒ Ⓓ

21. (A) deposit
(B) delivery
(C) contract
(D) survey

Ⓐ Ⓑ Ⓒ Ⓓ

22. (A) We cannot leave the package at your door.
(B) The cashier will accept credit cards.
(C) The workshop will finish at twelve o'clock.
(D) The special is Spanish cuisine.

Ⓐ Ⓑ Ⓒ Ⓓ

23. (A) at
(B) on
(C) in
(D) for

Ⓐ Ⓑ Ⓒ Ⓓ

Part 7 読解問題

文章を読んで、それぞれの設問の答えとして最も適切なものを１つずつ選びましょう。

Questions 24-26 refer to the following Web page.

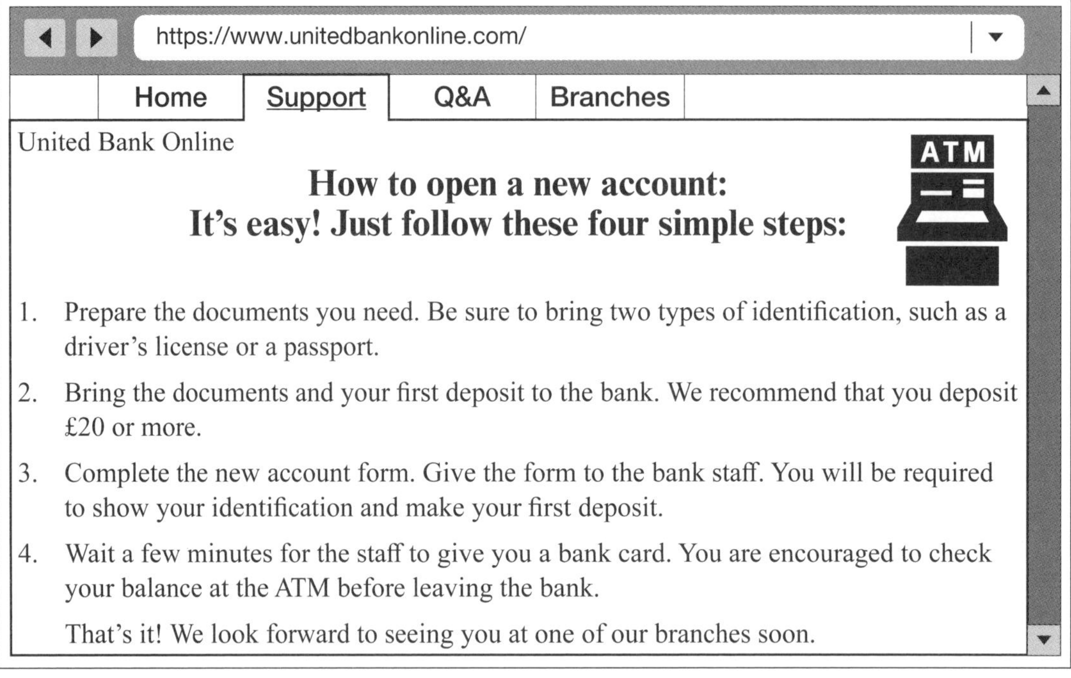

https://www.unitedbankonline.com/

Home | Support | Q&A | Branches

United Bank Online

How to open a new account:
It's easy! Just follow these four simple steps:

1. Prepare the documents you need. Be sure to bring two types of identification, such as a driver's license or a passport.
2. Bring the documents and your first deposit to the bank. We recommend that you deposit £20 or more.
3. Complete the new account form. Give the form to the bank staff. You will be required to show your identification and make your first deposit.
4. Wait a few minutes for the staff to give you a bank card. You are encouraged to check your balance at the ATM before leaving the bank.

That's it! We look forward to seeing you at one of our branches soon.

24. What kind of documents should customers bring to the bank?
(A) Certificates
(B) Contracts
(C) Budget documents
(D) Identification documents

Ⓐ Ⓑ Ⓒ Ⓓ

25. How long does it take for the bank to open a new account?
(A) A few minutes
(B) A few hours
(C) Three days
(D) One week

Ⓐ Ⓑ Ⓒ Ⓓ

26. What should customers do before they leave the bank?
(A) Open an envelope
(B) Check their balance
(C) Request a refund
(D) Send a package

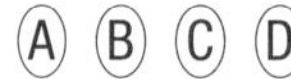

Job Hunting

就職活動

Word Bank

2-01

次のボキャブラリーの日本語の意味を(　　)内に書き、下のイラストのアルファベットを[　　]内に入れましょう。

① employee (　　　　) [　　]
② position (　　　　) [　　]
③ experience (　　　　) [　　]
④ interview (　　　　) [　　]
⑤ application (　　　　) [　　]
⑥ candidate (　　　　) [　　]
⑦ résumé (　　　　) [　　]
⑧ career (　　　　) [　　]
⑨ requirement (　　　　) [　　]
⑩ job opening (　　　　) [　　]

a.

b.

c.

d.

e.

f.

g.

h.

i.

j.
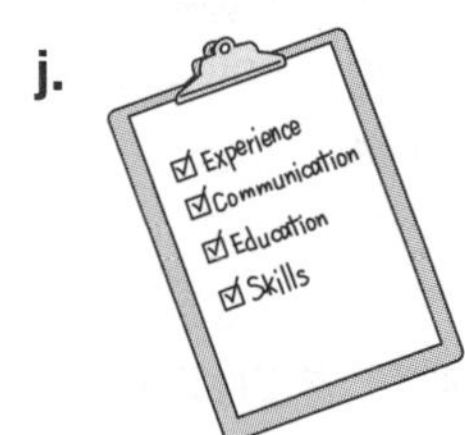

Listening Section

Let's Learn!

Part 2 応答問題　平叙文

平叙文とは、ピリオドで終わる文のことで、事実・情報・意見などを伝えます。応答はさまざまなので、内容をよく理解する必要があります。

平叙文1-3と応答a-cを読み、正しい応答を選びましょう。

1. I'm having trouble finding my glasses.　(　)
2. I hope that we'll have many applicants for the job.　(　)
3. I'm calling about my interview tomorrow.　(　)

a. May I ask your name, please?
b. I hope so, too.
c. They're on the desk.

Part 4 説明文問題　トークの種類―電話メッセージ（telephone message）―

電話メッセージでは、ビジネス関連の話題が取り上げられます。
①～③の項目に注目しましょう。

電話メッセージを見て、以下の問題に答えましょう。

① 話し手の名前　② 電話の用件

This is Mary Smith. I'm calling about the job opening we advertised. We have chosen five candidates for the position, and would like to interview them next week. I was wondering if you would attend the interviews. Please let me know when you are available.

③ 依頼や指示

1. 話し手の名前に下線を引きましょう。
2. 依頼内容に下線を引きましょう。

Let's Try!

Part 1 写真描写問題

2-02, 03

それぞれの写真について、4つの説明文のうち適切なものを１つずつ選びましょう。

1.

Ⓐ Ⓑ Ⓒ Ⓓ

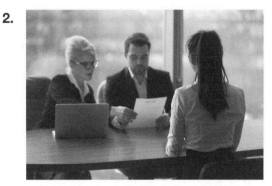

2.

Ⓐ Ⓑ Ⓒ Ⓓ

Part 2 応答問題

2-04~08

それぞれの質問の応答として最も適切なものを１つずつ選びましょう。

3. Mark your answer on your answer sheet. Ⓐ Ⓑ Ⓒ

4. Mark your answer on your answer sheet. Ⓐ Ⓑ Ⓒ

5. Mark your answer on your answer sheet. Ⓐ Ⓑ Ⓒ

6. Mark your answer on your answer sheet. Ⓐ Ⓑ Ⓒ

7. Mark your answer on your answer sheet. Ⓐ Ⓑ Ⓒ

Part 3 会話問題

2-09, 10

会話についての設問に対し、最も適切なものを１つずつ選びましょう。

8. What does the man want to do?
(A) Open an account
(B) Eat in a restaurant
(C) Get a new job
(D) Complete an assignment
Ⓐ Ⓑ Ⓒ Ⓓ

9. What job did the man have?
(A) Server
(B) Cashier
(C) Caterer
(D) Delivery driver
Ⓐ Ⓑ Ⓒ Ⓓ

10. What will the man probably do next?
(A) Visit a college campus
(B) Make a reservation
(C) Check his account balance
(D) Apply for the job
Ⓐ Ⓑ Ⓒ Ⓓ

Part 4 説明文問題

2-11, 12

説明文についての設問に対し、最も適切なものを１つずつ選びましょう。

11. What is the message about?
(A) A job opening
(B) A training workshop
(C) A company meeting
(D) A university seminar
Ⓐ Ⓑ Ⓒ Ⓓ

12. What will the speaker do next week?
(A) Send a résumé
(B) Take inventory
(C) Update a brochure
(D) Schedule interviews
Ⓐ Ⓑ Ⓒ Ⓓ

13. What does the speaker ask the listener to do?
(A) Reply with a good time for interviews
(B) Order new office equipment
(C) Send the budget information
(D) Send e-mails to customers
Ⓐ Ⓑ Ⓒ Ⓓ

Reading Section

Let's Learn!

Part 5 短文穴埋め問題 副詞

副詞（例文の**太字**）は、動詞、形容詞、副詞（下線部）に説明を加えるものです。選択肢の中で語尾に「-ly」がついているものは、副詞であることが多いです。

- 動詞を説明：He **quickly** solved the problem. / He solved the problem **quickly**.
- 形容詞を説明：The movie was **extremely** interesting.
- 副詞を説明：She sings **really** well.

（　　）のうち下線部を説明する語を選びましょう。

1. New employees have to sign their contracts (immediate / immediately).
2. The company has (recent / recently) updated its Web site.
3. You should send us an e-mail (quick / quickly).
4. We are (happy / happily) that there are some job openings at Alex Company.

Part 7 読解問題 文書の種類―求人広告―

求人広告とは、会社や店が、新しく人を雇うために出す広告のことです。①〜③の項目に注目しましょう。

求人広告を見て、下の問題の（ ）のうち正しいものを選びましょう。

① 募集する職種　② 応募条件

Gerald's Restaurant is hiring! We are looking for an assistant cook to work in our kitchens. Duties include preparing food and cleaning. Candidates should have some experience working in a restaurant. Please send your résumé to Gerald's Restaurant, 837 Grand Avenue, Glasston.

③ 応募方法

1. 募集されている職種は何ですか。　（シェフ / 清掃員）
2. 応募条件がありますか。　（ある / ない）
3. 応募するためには、何を送らなければなりませんか。　（手紙 / 履歴書）

Let's Try!

Part 5 短文穴埋め問題

それぞれの空所に入れるのに最も適切なものを1つずつ選びましょう。

14. New employees are required to sign their contracts no ------- than May 31.
(A) late
(B) later
(C) latest
(D) lately

Ⓐ Ⓑ Ⓒ Ⓓ

15. ------- you have any questions about our products, send us an e-mail.
(A) Would
(B) Could
(C) Should
(D) Might

Ⓐ Ⓑ Ⓒ Ⓓ

16. The company has ------- the requirements for new candidates.
(A) update
(B) updates
(C) updated
(D) updating

Ⓐ Ⓑ Ⓒ Ⓓ

17. I'm writing to ------- for the position of inventory manager.
(A) apply
(B) application
(C) applied
(D) applying

Ⓐ Ⓑ Ⓒ Ⓓ

18. Please note that candidates should complete the application -------.
(A) commonly
(B) lately
(C) suddenly
(D) immediately

Ⓐ Ⓑ Ⓒ Ⓓ

19. All employees are encouraged ------- fill out the survey.
(A) to
(B) for
(C) on
(D) in

Ⓐ Ⓑ Ⓒ Ⓓ

Part 6 長文穴埋め問題

それぞれの空所に入れるのに最も適切なものを１つずつ選びましょう。

Questions 20-23 refer to the following letter.

Global Ventures
Human Resources Department

502 First Avenue
Trandington, CA 99106

Gary Jones:

Thank you for your -------(**20.**) for the intern position at Global Ventures. We have now completed all of the interviews. We are happy -------(**21.**) inform you that you have been chosen for the position. -------(**22.**). We look forward to -------(**23.**) with you this summer.

Samantha Cooper
HR Manager

20. (A) employee
(B) shipment
(C) application
(D) refund

Ⓐ Ⓑ Ⓒ Ⓓ

21. (A) so
(B) by
(C) in
(D) to

Ⓐ Ⓑ Ⓒ Ⓓ

22. (A) Please take a moment to try the specials in the café.
(B) We hope that your intern experience will help to start your career in marketing.
(C) I'd like to call your attention to the photographs on the desk.
(D) We suggest that you send your résumé to a different company.

Ⓐ Ⓑ Ⓒ Ⓓ

23. (A) work
(B) works
(C) worked
(D) working

Ⓐ Ⓑ Ⓒ Ⓓ

Part 7 読解問題

文章を読んで、それぞれの設問の答えとして最も適切なものを１つずつ選びましょう。

Questions 24-26 refer to the following advertisement.

Gerald's Restaurant is hiring!

We are looking for an assistant cook to work in our kitchens. Duties include preparing food and cleaning. This is an entry-level position, but candidates should have some experience working in a restaurant. Cooking school graduates are encouraged to apply. Please send your résumé to Gerald's Restaurant, 837 Grand Avenue, Glasston. Please note that résumés will not be returned.

24. What is indicated about the job?
(A) It offers seminars.
(B) It includes preparing food.
(C) It is available only to experienced event planners.
(D) It requires a certificate in catering.

Ⓐ Ⓑ Ⓒ Ⓓ

25. What is required of job candidates?
(A) Completion of a special workshop
(B) Completion of an online application
(C) Experience as a cashier
(D) Experience working in a restaurant

Ⓐ Ⓑ Ⓒ Ⓓ

26. How should people apply for the job?
(A) Call the company headquarters
(B) Complete an application
(C) Send a résumé
(D) Visit the restaurant manager

Ⓐ Ⓑ Ⓒ Ⓓ

Housing
ハウジング

Word Bank

次のボキャブラリーの日本語の意味を(　　)内に書き、下のイラストのアルファベットを[　　]内に入れましょう。

① furniture (　　　　　　　　) [　　　]
② apartment (　　　　　　　　) [　　　]
③ rent (　　　　　　　　) [　　　]
④ resident (　　　　　　　　) [　　　]
⑤ real estate agent (　　　　　　　　) [　　　]
⑥ garage (　　　　　　　　) [　　　]
⑦ neighborhood (　　　　　　　　) [　　　]
⑧ property (　　　　　　　　) [　　　]
⑨ utility (　　　　　　　　) [　　　]
⑩ tenant (　　　　　　　　) [　　　]

Listening Section

Let's Learn!

Part 1 写真描写問題 人物の行動を表す動詞

人物の行動を表す動詞にはさまざまなものがあります。
現在進行形（be 動詞＋動詞の -ing 形）とともによく登場します。
water（～に水をやる）、face（～の方を向く）、lean（～にもたれる）、adjust（～を調整する）、load（～を積む）、board（～に搭乗する）、stack/pile（～を積み重ねる）などがよく出題されます。

(　　) のうち写真に合うものを選びましょう。

1. The woman is (watering / loading) some plants.

2. The man is (adjusting / stacking) the air conditioner.

3. A woman is (facing / boarding) the display case.

Part 3 会話問題 森問題—場所—

「会話が行われている場所」を問う問題は森問題です。会話全体に答えのヒントが散らばっています。Where most likely are the speakers?（話し手はどこにいると考えられますか）Where most likely is the conversation taking place?（会話はどこで行われていると考えられますか）などの質問で問われます。

以下の会話文は、場所を問う問題のヒントのみを残し、それ以外の単語を消しています。

Man: Welcome __ Regal Realty. ____________?
Woman: ______, I'm looking ______ new apartment.
Man: ______, ______ would you like to live in?
Woman: I'd like to live close ______.

場所を問う質問文：Where most likely are the speakers? (　　)
これを見て、下の問題のa-cのうち正しいものを選びましょう。

a. 不動産業者のオフィス　**b.** 教室　**c.** 郵便局

Let's Try!

Part 1 写真描写問題

2-14, 15

それぞれの写真について、4つの説明文のうち適切なものを１つずつ選びましょう。

1.

Ⓐ Ⓑ Ⓒ Ⓓ

2.

Ⓐ Ⓑ Ⓒ Ⓓ

Part 2 応答問題

2-16~20

それぞれの質問の応答として最も適切なものを１つずつ選びましょう。

3. Mark your answer on your answer sheet. Ⓐ Ⓑ Ⓒ

4. Mark your answer on your answer sheet. Ⓐ Ⓑ Ⓒ

5. Mark your answer on your answer sheet. Ⓐ Ⓑ Ⓒ

6. Mark your answer on your answer sheet. Ⓐ Ⓑ Ⓒ

7. Mark your answer on your answer sheet. Ⓐ Ⓑ Ⓒ

Part 3 会話問題

2-21, 22

会話についての設問に対し、最も適切なものを１つずつ選びましょう。

8. Where most likely is the conversation taking place?
(A) A real estate agent's office
(B) A bank branch
(C) A post office
(D) A museum box office

Ⓐ Ⓑ Ⓒ Ⓓ

9. What does the man mean when he says, "Why don't you take a look at this one"?
(A) He thinks the property is expensive.
(B) He is suggesting an inventory check.
(C) He wants to move into an apartment.
(D) He is suggesting a visit to an apartment.

Ⓐ Ⓑ Ⓒ Ⓓ

10. Why does the woman want a big apartment?
(A) She has children.
(B) She has a lot of furniture.
(C) She works from home.
(D) She has a cat.

Ⓐ Ⓑ Ⓒ Ⓓ

Part 4 説明文問題

2-23, 24

説明文についての設問に対し、最も適切なものを１つずつ選びましょう。

11. Who are the listeners for the talk?
(A) Store supervisors
(B) Hotel guests
(C) Apartment tenants
(D) Event caterers

Ⓐ Ⓑ Ⓒ Ⓓ

12. What does the speaker ask the listeners to do?
(A) Move their furniture
(B) Make a reservation
(C) Send a document
(D) Put their bicycles in the garage

Ⓐ Ⓑ Ⓒ Ⓓ

13. What will the speaker do next week?
(A) Send a document
(B) Make a request
(C) Buy a bicycle
(D) Call a real estate agent

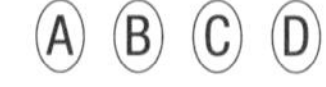

Reading Section

Let's Learn!

Part 5 短文穴埋め問題　動名詞・不定詞

以下の動詞は、次に続く動詞の形が決まっています。
①動名詞（動詞＋ -ing）が続く動詞：
enjoy, consider, mind, suggest, keep, avoid, deny
②不定詞（to ＋動詞の原形）が続く動詞：
want, expect, hesitate, plan, manage, schedule

（　　　）のうち正しいものを選びましょう。

1. We enjoyed (living / to live) in the apartment.
2. Mr. Park suggested (visiting / to visit) the real estate agent.
3. Please do not hesitate (to ask / asking) questions.
4. The train to Boston is scheduled (to leave / leaving) in an hour.

Part 7 読解問題　文書の種類― E-mail ―

E メールは、本文以外にも受信者・送信者・件名・日付にも正解のヒントが書かれています。本文の内容は仕事のスケジュールや商品に関するクレームなど多岐にわたります。

Eメールを見て、下の問題の（　　）のうち正しいものを選びましょう。

To: Geraldine Conners <gconners@ionly.com>
From: James Atkins <jatkins@abcrealtor.com>
Date: February 13
Subject: Apartment in your budget

To: 受信者
From: 送信者
Date: 日付
Subject: 件名

② 用件

Dear Ms. Conners,

① メールの受信者

I am happy to inform you that I found an apartment in your budget. It is in a quiet neighborhood and has a garage on the property. Please take a moment to look at the document and let me know if you want to see the apartment.

Best regards,
James Atkins

1. このメールの受信者は誰ですか。　(Geraldine Conners / James Atkins)
2. 用件は何ですか。　(アパートについて / 駐車場について)
3. 送信者の職業は何ですか。　(不動産業者 / 会社の人事担当)

Let's Try!

Part 5 短文穴埋め問題

それぞれの空所に入れるのに最も適切なものを１つずつ選びましょう。

14. Be ------- to send a new tenant application by May 16.
(A) rare
(B) pure
(C) severe
(D) sure
Ⓐ Ⓑ Ⓒ Ⓓ

15. Should you have any questions, please contact us before ------- the rent.
(A) pay
(B) pays
(C) paid
(D) paying
Ⓐ Ⓑ Ⓒ Ⓓ

16. If you need to find a new apartment quickly, please consider ------- our office.
(A) visiting
(B) to visit
(C) visited
(D) visits
Ⓐ Ⓑ Ⓒ Ⓓ

17. Ms. Maxwell is responsible ------- managing properties.
(A) for
(B) in
(C) to
(D) with
Ⓐ Ⓑ Ⓒ Ⓓ

18. Our real estate ------- can be reached at 555-0218.
(A) another
(B) agent
(C) agenda
(D) angel
Ⓐ Ⓑ Ⓒ Ⓓ

19. Please note that this ------- is not available for purchase.
(A) properly
(B) proper
(C) property
(D) properties
Ⓐ Ⓑ Ⓒ Ⓓ

Part 6 長文穴埋め問題

それぞれの空所に入れるのに最も適切なものを１つずつ選びましょう。

Questions 20-23 refer to the following notice.

Do you want some new things to refresh your apartment? Do you ------- (20.) extra things you don't need? Come to the San Trego neighborhood sale on May 15! All ------- (21.) are encouraged to bring their used items to sell. You can even bring large items like cabinets and shelves! Anyone can buy things ------- (22.) the sale, so many people might come. -------. (23.) Be sure to call Mary Simmons at 555-1873 to sign up.

20. (A) are
(B) has
(C) have
(D) is

Ⓐ Ⓑ Ⓒ Ⓓ

21. (A) campuses
(B) residents
(C) purchases
(D) deliveries

Ⓐ Ⓑ Ⓒ Ⓓ

22. (A) at
(B) by
(C) on
(D) of

Ⓐ Ⓑ Ⓒ Ⓓ

23. (A) The seminar will be two weeks long.
(B) The winner will receive a small prize.
(C) The first performance is at 8:00 P.M.
(D) It is a good chance to get money for your old things.

Ⓐ Ⓑ Ⓒ Ⓓ

Part 7 読解問題

文章を読んで、それぞれの設問の答えとして最も適切なものを１つずつ選びましょう。

Questions 24-27 refer to the following e-mail.

E-Mail Message

To:	Geraldine Conners <gconners@ionly.com>
From:	James Atkins <jatkins@abcrealtor.com>
Date:	February 13
Subject:	Three apartments in your budget

Dear Ms. Conners,

I am happy to inform you that I found three apartments in your budget. The first one is in a quiet neighborhood and has a garage on the property. – [1] –. The second one is in a busy neighborhood and utilities are included in the rent. – [2] –. The third apartment is in a building with friendly tenants who often organize events. – [3] –. Please take a moment to look at the document and let me know if you want to see any of the apartments. – [4] –.

James Atkins

24. What most likely is Mr. Atkins' job?
(A) A store cashier
(B) A construction worker
(C) A real estate agent
(D) A tour guide

Ⓐ Ⓑ Ⓒ Ⓓ

25. What is the e-mail mainly about?
(A) Vacation plans
(B) Office buildings for sale
(C) Bank accounts
(D) Apartments for rent

Ⓐ Ⓑ Ⓒ Ⓓ

26. What does Mr. Atkins ask Ms. Conners to do?
(A) Look at a document
(B) Fill in a survey
(C) Open an account
(D) Attend an event

Ⓐ Ⓑ Ⓒ Ⓓ

27. In which of the positions marked [1], [2], [3], and [4] does the following sentence best belong?

"I have attached a document with the details of each apartment."

(A) [1]
(B) [2]
(C) [3]
(D) [4]

Ⓐ Ⓑ Ⓒ Ⓓ

Transportation

交通

Word Bank

次のボキャブラリーの日本語の意味を(　　)内に書き、下のイラストのアルファベットを[　　]内に入れましょう。

① schedule (　　　　　　　　　　) [　　　　]
② flight (　　　　　　　　　　) [　　　　]
③ weather (　　　　　　　　　　) [　　　　]
④ passenger (　　　　　　　　　　) [　　　　]
⑤ delay (　　　　　　　　　　) [　　　　]
⑥ arrival (　　　　　　　　　　) [　　　　]
⑦ route (　　　　　　　　　　) [　　　　]
⑧ destination (　　　　　　　　　　) [　　　　]
⑨ fare (　　　　　　　　　　) [　　　　]
⑩ departure (　　　　　　　　　　) [　　　　]

Listening Section

Let's Learn!

Part 2　応答問題　―依頼・申し出―

依頼や申し出に対する応答にはパターンがあります。

以下の質問は依頼ですか、申し出ですか。どちらかを選びましょう。

1. Could you help me with my sales report?　（依頼 / 申し出）
受ける：Sure. / OK.（いいですよ。）
断る　：Sorry, but I'm busy.（ごめんなさい、忙しいのです。）

2. Shall I help you with your sales report?　（依頼 / 申し出）
受ける：I'd appreciate that.（ありがたいです。）
断る　：Thanks, but I can manage.（ありがとう、でも自分でできます。）

Part 4　説明文問題　トークの種類―アナウンス（announcement）―

アナウンスは空港、店内、駅、美術館などで聞かれます。アナウンスを聞いた人が次にとる行動がよく出題されます。

アナウンスの一部を見て、以下の問題に答えましょう。

② 対象者　① 詳細

Attention all passengers. Because of bad weather, Flight 732 will leave at 2:45 not 1:30. Please go to the boarding gate at least 15 minutes before departure.

③ 次の行動

1. アナウンスの対象者に下線を引きましょう。
2. アナウンスの対象者が次にとる行動に下線を引きましょう。

Let's Try!

Part 1 写真描写問題

2-26, 27

それぞれの写真について、4つの説明文のうち適切なものを１つずつ選びましょう。

1.

Ⓐ Ⓑ Ⓒ Ⓓ

2.

Ⓐ Ⓑ Ⓒ Ⓓ

Part 2 応答問題

2-28~32

それぞれの質問の応答として最も適切なものを１つずつ選びましょう。

3. Mark your answer on your answer sheet. Ⓐ Ⓑ Ⓒ

4. Mark your answer on your answer sheet. Ⓐ Ⓑ Ⓒ

5. Mark your answer on your answer sheet. Ⓐ Ⓑ Ⓒ

6. Mark your answer on your answer sheet. Ⓐ Ⓑ Ⓒ

7. Mark your answer on your answer sheet. Ⓐ Ⓑ Ⓒ

Part 3 会話問題

2-33, 34

会話についての設問に対し、最も適切なものを１つずつ選びましょう。

8. What is the conversation mostly about?
(A) A seminar deadline
(B) Passengers on a flight
(C) Vacation destinations
(D) A travel plan

Ⓐ Ⓑ Ⓒ Ⓓ

9. What does the woman ask the men to do?
(A) Deliver a package
(B) Call a client
(C) Help her choose a train route
(D) Update a brochure

Ⓐ Ⓑ Ⓒ Ⓓ

10. Which route will the woman take?
(A) The fastest one
(B) The slow one
(C) The one with a special menu
(D) The one with a garage

Ⓐ Ⓑ Ⓒ Ⓓ

Part 4 説明文問題

2-35, 36

説明文についての設問に対し、最も適切なものを１つずつ選びましょう。

11. Why is the plane late?
(A) It is a new route.
(B) The fare changed.
(C) The passengers were late.
(D) There is bad weather.

Ⓐ Ⓑ Ⓒ Ⓓ

12. When will the plane leave?
(A) 1:30 P.M.
(B) 2:45 P.M.
(C) 7:32 P.M.
(D) 7:45 P.M.

Ⓐ Ⓑ Ⓒ Ⓓ

13. What does the speaker ask the passengers to do?
(A) Get a refund
(B) Take a different flight
(C) Go to the boarding gate
(D) Ask for a coupon

Ⓐ Ⓑ Ⓒ Ⓓ

Reading Section

Let's Learn!

Part 5 短文穴埋め問題　接続詞①—文と文をつなぐ語句—

接続詞は 1 つの節（主語＋動詞）と別の節をつなぎます。次の 2 種類のつなぎ方があります。

1. 節＋**接続詞**＋節.
2. **接続詞**＋節，節.

次の接続詞が共通して表す意味を選びましょう。

1. because, since　（逆説・理由・とき・条件）
2. although, (even) though, while　（逆説・理由・とき・条件）
3. if, unless　（逆説・理由・とき・条件）
4. when, once　（逆説・理由・とき・条件）

Part 7 読解問題　文書の種類—複数の文書に関する問題①（解き方のヒント）—

複数の文書に関する問題とは、2 つまたは 3 つの関連した文書を読み設問に答えるものです。1 つの文書だけを読めば解ける設問と、2 つの文書を読まないと解けない設問があります。1 つの文書だけを読めば解ける設問には、文書の種類が入っていることが多いです。
例：According to the e-mail, …（E メールによると…）In the e-mail, …（E メールでは…）

文書の上にある案内文：
Questions 1-3 refer to the following e-mail and schedule.

1 つの文書だけを読めば解ける設問に ✓ を入れましょう。

According to the schedule, what time does the flight to London depart?　(　)
Where will Ms. Simmons meet Ms. Abbot?　(　)
What is the purpose of the e-mail?　(　)

Let's Try!

Part 5 短文穴埋め問題

それぞれの空所に入れるのに最も適切なものを１つずつ選びましょう。

14. All passengers are required to show their passports ------- they board the flight.
(A) when
(B) so
(C) although
(D) unless
Ⓐ Ⓑ Ⓒ Ⓓ

15. The route will be updated ------- the supervisor approves it.
(A) at
(B) before
(C) until
(D) after
Ⓐ Ⓑ Ⓒ Ⓓ

16. Please ------- a moment to check the arrival time of your flight.
(A) get
(B) bring
(C) take
(D) carry
Ⓐ Ⓑ Ⓒ Ⓓ

17. We suggest that you ------- the bus driver about routes and destinations.
(A) will ask
(B) ask
(C) asked
(D) asking
Ⓐ Ⓑ Ⓒ Ⓓ

18. I am writing ------- the schedule for your flight on June 15.
(A) about
(B) of
(C) in
(D) at
Ⓐ Ⓑ Ⓒ Ⓓ

19. Should you ------- any questions about your arrival time, please call us.
(A) there
(B) are
(C) be
(D) have
Ⓐ Ⓑ Ⓒ Ⓓ

Part 6 長文穴埋め問題

それぞれの空所に入れるのに最も適切なものを１つずつ選びましょう。

Questions 20-23 refer to the following advertisement.

Azure Air
Announcing 3 new routes!

Azure Air is now flying to three exciting new -------! (20.) To celebrate our new routes, all passengers flying to New York, London, and Minneapolis can ------- (21.) a 20% discount off the regular fare! -------. (22.) We offer a great service for a great price! We look forward to flying ------- (23.) you!

20. (A) delays
(B) flights
(C) shipments
(D) destinations

Ⓐ Ⓑ Ⓒ Ⓓ

21. (A) get
(B) gets
(C) got
(D) have gotten

Ⓐ Ⓑ Ⓒ Ⓓ

22. (A) You are encouraged to volunteer for the neighborhood event.
(B) We apologize for the delayed arrival of your flight.
(C) Please take a moment to look at our flight schedule.
(D) Please note that construction will begin next week.

Ⓐ Ⓑ Ⓒ Ⓓ

23. (A) to
(B) with
(C) on
(D) through

Ⓐ Ⓑ Ⓒ Ⓓ

Part 7 読解問題

文章を読んで、それぞれの設問の答えとして最も適切なものを１つずつ選びましょう。

Questions 24-28 refer to the following e-mail and schedule.

E-Mail Message

To: Margaret Simmons <Simmons1@helpful.com>
From: Jane Abbot <Abbotj@acecater.com>
Date: August 10
Subject: Arriving home on Tuesday!

Margaret:

Thank you for agreeing to meet me at the airport next Tuesday. I had a great vacation, but I am excited to go home again. I would appreciate it if you could meet me in the arrivals area. I will be on flight GX145 from Paris. I should arrive at 6:00 P.M., but be sure to check the online schedule to see if there are any delays. I look forward to seeing you then!

Best regards,
Jane

Metro Airport Flight Schedule

Departures

Flight	To		Departure Time
NM634	**London**	on time	5:30
FB933	**Amsterdam**	delayed	6:00
GX289	**Milan**	delayed	6:15
NM812	**Frankfurt**	on time	7:30

Arrivals

Flight	From		Estimated Arrival Time
RG332	**St. Petersburg**	on time	5:45
NM128	**Frankfurt**	on time	6:20
GX145	**Paris**	delayed	7:15
FB602	**Amsterdam**	delayed	7:45

24. What is the purpose of the e-mail?
(A) To confirm a schedule
(B) To reserve a flight
(C) To reschedule an appointment
(D) To make a reservation

Ⓐ Ⓑ Ⓒ Ⓓ

25. What will Ms. Simmons most likely do on Tuesday?
(A) Buy a ticket for an art exhibition
(B) Go on vacation with Ms. Abbot
(C) Meet Ms. Abbot at the airport
(D) Interview Ms. Abbot for a job

Ⓐ Ⓑ Ⓒ Ⓓ

26. In the e-mail, the word "excited" in paragraph, line 2, is closest in meaning to
(A) disappointed
(B) delighted
(C) surprised
(D) amazed

Ⓐ Ⓑ Ⓒ Ⓓ

27. Where will Ms. Simmons meet Ms. Abbot?
(A) The arrivals area of the airport
(B) The departure area of the airport
(C) The main entrance of the art museum
(D) The headquarters of the company

Ⓐ Ⓑ Ⓒ Ⓓ

28. What time should Ms. Simmons go to the arrival area?
(A) 1:45 P.M.
(B) 6:00 P.M.
(C) 6:30 P.M.
(D) 7:15 P.M.

Ⓐ Ⓑ Ⓒ Ⓓ

Hotels

ホテル

Word Bank

次のボキャブラリーの日本語の意味を(　　)内に書き、下のイラストのアルファベットを[　　]内に入れましょう。

① guest (　　　　) [　　]
② renovation (　　　　) [　　]
③ reception (　　　　) [　　]
④ lobby (　　　　) [　　]
⑤ banquet (　　　　) [　　]
⑥ complaint (　　　　) [　　]
⑦ shuttle (　　　　) [　　]
⑧ check-in (　　　　) [　　]
⑨ accommodation (　　　　) [　　]
⑩ laundry (　　　　) [　　]

a.

b.

c.

d.
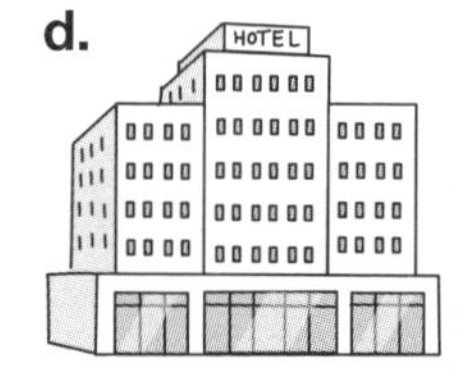

e.

f.

g.

h.

i.

j.

Listening Section

Let's Learn!

Part 2 応答問題 ―提案・勧誘―

提案・勧誘の応答には定型表現がよく使用されます。

以下の提案や勧誘を表す英文例の応答として正しい方を選びましょう。

・提案：（相手が）受付でバスのスケジュールを確認する。
英文例 1 ：Why don't you check the bus schedule at the reception desk?
英文例 2 ：You should check the bus schedule at the reception desk.
応答：（Because I don't. / That's a good idea.）

・勧誘：（話し手と相手が一緒に）あとで洗濯する。
英文例 1 ：Shall we do the laundry later?
英文例 2 ：Why don't we do the laundry later?
英文例 3 ：Let's do the laundry later.
応答：（Yes, let's. / No, I don't.）

Part 3 会話問題 ―木問題―

森問題とは異なり、木問題はピンポイントの情報を問う設問です。よく出題される定型的な設問がありますので、設問をあらかじめ読んでおき、答えを待ち伏せしましょう。以下のような設問がよく出題されます。

以下の木問題を読み、正しい日本語訳を選びましょう。

1. What is the problem? (　)
2. Why is the woman calling? (　)
3. What does the man suggest? (　)
4. What does the man request? (　)
5. What will the man most likely do next? (　)

a. 男性は何を提案していますか。　b. 女性はなぜ電話をしていますか。
c. 問題は何ですか。　d. 男性は何を求めていますか。
e . 男性は次に何をすると考えられますか。

Let's Try!

Part 1 写真描写問題

2-38, 39

それぞれの写真について、4つの説明文のうち適切なものを1つずつ選びましょう。

1. Ⓐ Ⓑ Ⓒ Ⓓ

2. 

Ⓐ Ⓑ Ⓒ Ⓓ

Part 2 応答問題

2-40~44

それぞれの質問の応答として最も適切なものを1つずつ選びましょう。

3. Mark your answer on your answer sheet. Ⓐ Ⓑ Ⓒ

4. Mark your answer on your answer sheet. Ⓐ Ⓑ Ⓒ

5. Mark your answer on your answer sheet. Ⓐ Ⓑ Ⓒ

6. Mark your answer on your answer sheet. Ⓐ Ⓑ Ⓒ

7. Mark your answer on your answer sheet. Ⓐ Ⓑ Ⓒ

Part 3 会話問題

会話についての設問に対し、最も適切なものを１つずつ選びましょう。

8. What most likely is the man's job?
(A) Bank manager
(B) Restaurant server
(C) Hotel clerk
(D) Construction worker

Ⓐ Ⓑ Ⓒ Ⓓ

9. What time can the woman go to her hotel room?
(A) 6:00 A.M.
(B) 9:00 A.M.
(C) 12:00 P.M.
(D) 2:00 P.M.

Ⓐ Ⓑ Ⓒ Ⓓ

10. What does the woman say she must do tomorrow?
(A) Do laundry
(B) Go to the airport
(C) Drive a shuttle
(D) Attend a banquet

Ⓐ Ⓑ Ⓒ Ⓓ

Part 4 説明文問題

説明文についての設問に対し、最も適切なものを１つずつ選びましょう。

Breakfast Coupon

Japanese breakfast	Sakura Restaurant	8:30-10:00 A.M.
English breakfast	Grand Café	8:30-10:00 A.M.
Buffet	Iris Banquet Hall	6:00-8:30 A.M.

11. Who is the speaker talking to?
(A) Caterers
(B) Hotel staff
(C) A tour group
(D) A theater audience

Ⓐ Ⓑ Ⓒ Ⓓ

12. Look at the graphic. What kind of breakfast will the listeners be served?
(A) Buffet
(B) Japanese
(C) English
(D) Chinese

Ⓐ Ⓑ Ⓒ Ⓓ

13. Where does the speaker ask the listeners to meet?
(A) By the theater box office
(B) In the hotel lobby
(C) In the laundry room
(D) In the restaurant kitchen

Ⓐ Ⓑ Ⓒ Ⓓ

Reading Section

Let's Learn!

Part 5 短文穴埋め問題　接続詞②―前置詞 / 接続詞―

接続詞の後には節が、前置詞 / 群前置詞※の後には名詞（句）が続きます。節は主語＋動詞のことで、名詞（句）は 2 語以上の語のかたまりで、名詞の役割を果たします。

※群前置詞＝前置詞の働きをする 2 語以上の句

次の表の空所に入る語を下の語群から選び、完成させましょう。

	接続詞	前置詞
理由（～なので）	because	
期間（～の間に）		during
譲歩（～にもかかわらず・～であるけれども）	although	

in spite of　　while　　because of

Part 7 読解問題　文書の種類―複数の文書に関する問題②（解き方のヒント）―

複数の文書に関する問題とは、2 つまたは 3 つの関連した文書を読み設問に答えるものです。出題される文書には色々な組み合わせがあります。

次の指示文を読み、文書の種類に下線を引きましょう。

1. Questions 1-3 refer to the following e-mail and schedule.

2. Questions 1-3 refer to the following advertisement and application.

3. Questions 1-3 refer to the following Web site, e-mail, and coupon.

Let's Try!

Part 5 短文穴埋め問題

それぞれの空所に入れるのに最も適切なものを１つずつ選びましょう。

14. ------- the renovation, the lobby will remain open.
(A) Because
(B) During
(C) While
(D) Even though — Ⓐ Ⓑ Ⓒ Ⓓ

15. Accommodation is hard to find ------- a conference this week.
(A) although
(B) because
(C) except
(D) because of — Ⓐ Ⓑ Ⓒ Ⓓ

16. Hotel assistant managers ------- deal with complaints from guests.
(A) does
(B) are
(C) will
(D) is — Ⓐ Ⓑ Ⓒ Ⓓ

17. We look forward ------- you again in the near future.
(A) service
(B) to serve
(C) to serving
(D) serving — Ⓐ Ⓑ Ⓒ Ⓓ

18. We are happy to ------- you that this year's award ceremony will be at a hotel banquet room.
(A) inform
(B) informing
(C) be informed
(D) informed — Ⓐ Ⓑ Ⓒ Ⓓ

19. ------- guests are encouraged to try the hotel spa during their stay.
(A) Our
(B) Ours
(C) Us
(D) Ourselves — Ⓐ Ⓑ Ⓒ Ⓓ

Part 6 長文穴埋め問題

それぞれの空所に入れるのに最も適切なものを１つずつ選びましょう。

Questions 20-23 refer to the following notice.

Welcome to the Alston Arms Inn

We hope you -------(20.) enjoy your stay with us. Please note that renovations have begun on the banquet hall. -------(21.). We are happy to inform you that our full menu is still available and you can enjoy our famous local cuisine. We are sure you won't have any complaints! We hope that all of our -------(22.) will have a comfortable stay. Should you have any requests, please call reception -------(23.) any time.

20. (A) are
(B) were
(C) will
(D) did

Ⓐ Ⓑ Ⓒ Ⓓ

21. (A) The shuttle route has changed, so there might be a delay.
(B) There is a grocery store in the neighborhood, so here are some coupons.
(C) The laundry room is on the third floor, so please wash your clothes.
(D) The area is under construction, so breakfast will be served in the lobby.

Ⓐ Ⓑ Ⓒ Ⓓ

22. (A) guests
(B) orders
(C) headquarters
(D) candidates

Ⓐ Ⓑ Ⓒ Ⓓ

23. (A) in
(B) on
(C) at
(D) by

Ⓐ Ⓑ Ⓒ Ⓓ

Part 7 読解問題

文章を読んで、それぞれの設問の答えとして最も適切なものを1つずつ選びましょう。

Questions 24-28 refer to the following Web page and e-mail.

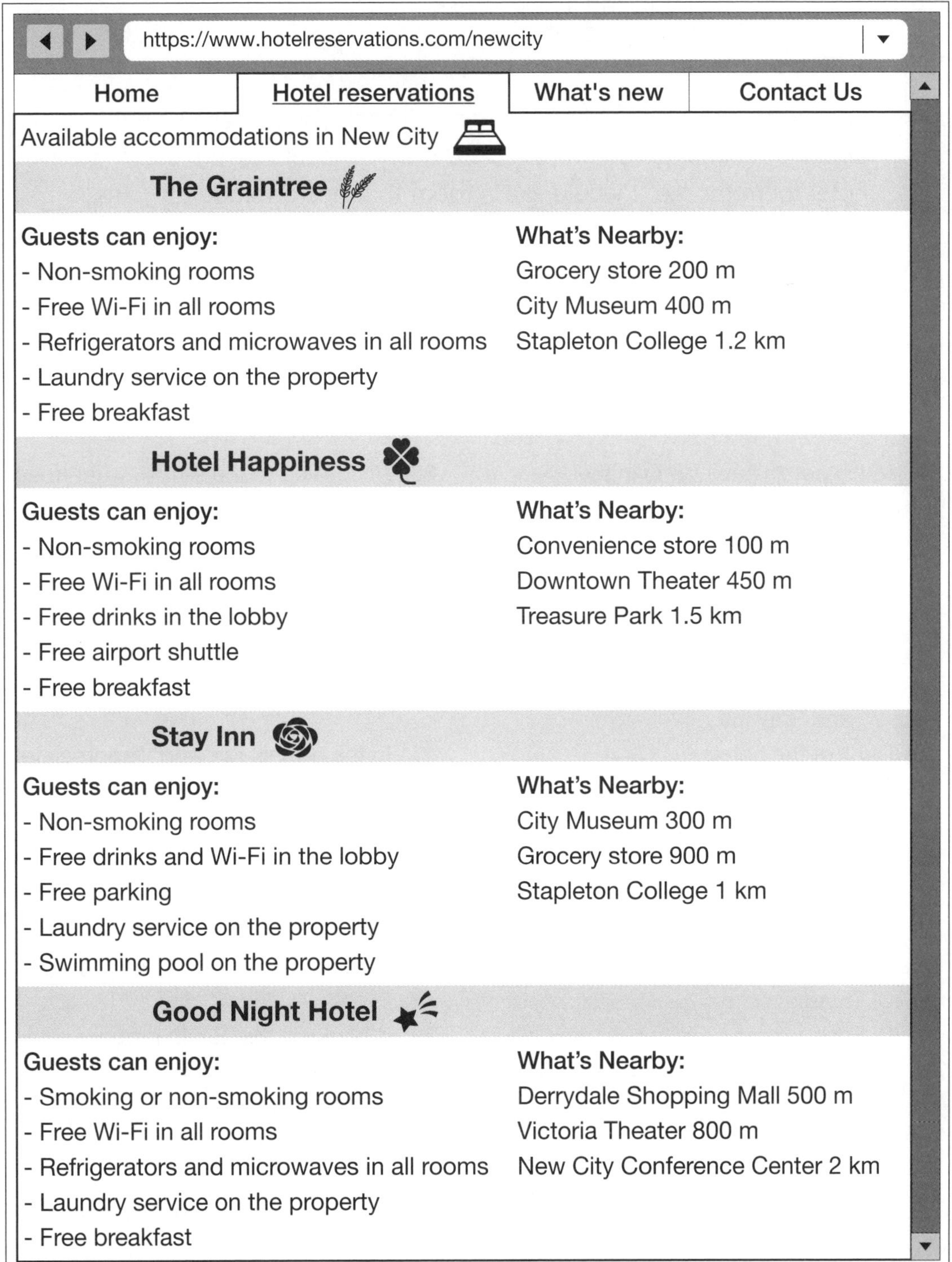

https://www.hotelreservations.com/newcity

Home | Hotel reservations | What's new | Contact Us

Available accommodations in New City

The Graintree

Guests can enjoy:
- Non-smoking rooms
- Free Wi-Fi in all rooms
- Refrigerators and microwaves in all rooms
- Laundry service on the property
- Free breakfast

What's Nearby:
Grocery store 200 m
City Museum 400 m
Stapleton College 1.2 km

Hotel Happiness

Guests can enjoy:
- Non-smoking rooms
- Free Wi-Fi in all rooms
- Free drinks in the lobby
- Free airport shuttle
- Free breakfast

What's Nearby:
Convenience store 100 m
Downtown Theater 450 m
Treasure Park 1.5 km

Stay Inn

Guests can enjoy:
- Non-smoking rooms
- Free drinks and Wi-Fi in the lobby
- Free parking
- Laundry service on the property
- Swimming pool on the property

What's Nearby:
City Museum 300 m
Grocery store 900 m
Stapleton College 1 km

Good Night Hotel

Guests can enjoy:
- Smoking or non-smoking rooms
- Free Wi-Fi in all rooms
- Refrigerators and microwaves in all rooms
- Laundry service on the property
- Free breakfast

What's Nearby:
Derrydale Shopping Mall 500 m
Victoria Theater 800 m
New City Conference Center 2 km

E-Mail Message

To:	Courtney Smith <Smith_C@travelbest.com>
From:	Albert Jones <ajones318@history.edu>
Date:	May 26
Subject:	New City Hotel Reservation

Dear Ms. Smith,

I am writing about my trip next month. Thank you for reserving the airplane tickets. I would appreciate it if you could also reserve a hotel room for me. I would like a room that has a refrigerator and Wi-Fi. Please note that I need to stay in a hotel near the museum. It would be nice if the hotel has a laundry service and free breakfast.

Best regards,
Albert Jones

24. Which hotels have Wi-Fi in the rooms?
(A) Hotel Happiness, Stay Inn, and Good Night Hotel
(B) The Graintree, Hotel Happiness, and Good Night Hotel
(C) The Graintree, Hotel Happiness, and Stay Inn
(D) All of the hotels

Ⓐ Ⓑ Ⓒ Ⓓ

25. How many hotels have non-smoking rooms available?
(A) One
(B) Two
(C) Three
(D) Four

Ⓐ Ⓑ Ⓒ Ⓓ

26. According to the e-mail, what does Mr. Jones need to do?
(A) Wash his clothes
(B) Keep his food cold
(C) Write e-mails
(D) Stay near the museum

Ⓐ Ⓑ Ⓒ Ⓓ

27. In the e-mail, the word "appreciate" in paragraph, line 2, is closest in meaning to
(A) make
(B) thank
(C) understand
(D) cancel

Ⓐ Ⓑ Ⓒ Ⓓ

28. Where will Ms. Smith probably reserve a hotel room?
(A) The Graintree
(B) Hotel Happiness
(C) Stay Inn
(D) Good Night Hotel

Ⓐ Ⓑ Ⓒ Ⓓ

Events

イベント

Word Bank

次のボキャブラリーの日本語の意味を(　　)内に書き、下のイラストのアルファベットを[　　]内に入れましょう。

① location (　　　　) [　　]
② program (　　　　) [　　]
③ training (　　　　) [　　]
④ award (　　　　) [　　]
⑤ participant (　　　　) [　　]
⑥ launch (　　　　) [　　]
⑦ promotion (　　　　) [　　]
⑧ ceremony (　　　　) [　　]
⑨ retirement (　　　　) [　　]
⑩ anniversary (　　　　) [　　]

Listening Section

Let's Learn!

Part 1 写真描写問題 ―受動態―

ものが主語の場合、受動態（be 動詞＋過去分詞）が用いられることがあります。

(　　) のうち写真に合うものを選びましょう。

1. Chairs are (placed / bought) around the tables.

2. Tables are (arranged / broken) in the room.

Part 4 説明文問題 トークの種類―会議の一部②（excerpt from a meeting）―

会議の一部は、社員への連絡事項やビジネス関連の話題が取り上げられます。

会議の一部を見て、以下の問題に答えましょう。

Good afternoon, everyone. First, I'm pleased to announce that we are starting a new training program. Participants in the program will be candidates for promotion to supervisor positions. I'm afraid that only six people can join the program, so you are encouraged to apply early.

1. 会議の話題に下線を引きましょう。
2. 指示内容に下線を引きましょう。

Let's Try!

Part 1 写真描写問題

2-50, 51

それぞれの写真について、4つの説明文のうち適切なものを１つずつ選びましょう。

1.

Ⓐ Ⓑ Ⓒ Ⓓ

2.

Ⓐ Ⓑ Ⓒ Ⓓ

Part 2 応答問題

2-52~56

それぞれの質問の応答として最も適切なものを１つずつ選びましょう。

3. Mark your answer on your answer sheet. Ⓐ Ⓑ Ⓒ

4. Mark your answer on your answer sheet. Ⓐ Ⓑ Ⓒ

5. Mark your answer on your answer sheet. Ⓐ Ⓑ Ⓒ

6. Mark your answer on your answer sheet. Ⓐ Ⓑ Ⓒ

7. Mark your answer on your answer sheet. Ⓐ Ⓑ Ⓒ

Part 3 会話問題

会話についての設問に対し、最も適切なものを１つずつ選びましょう。

8. What is the conversation mainly about?
(A) A product launch
(B) An award ceremony
(C) A retirement party
(D) A company anniversary
Ⓐ Ⓑ Ⓒ Ⓓ

9. Where will the event be held?
(A) A theater
(B) A hotel
(C) A college campus
(D) The company headquarters
Ⓐ Ⓑ Ⓒ Ⓓ

10. What will the man most likely do next?
(A) Contact the caterer
(B) Retire
(C) Invite some guests
(D) Attend a training seminar
Ⓐ Ⓑ Ⓒ Ⓓ

Part 4 説明文問題

説明文についての設問に対し、最も適切なものを１つずつ選びましょう。

11. Who are the listeners?
(A) Apartment residents
(B) Hotel guests
(C) Airplane passengers
(D) Company employees
Ⓐ Ⓑ Ⓒ Ⓓ

12. What will be starting next month?
(A) An office renovation
(B) A product promotion
(C) A training program
(D) A research project
Ⓐ Ⓑ Ⓒ Ⓓ

13. What does the speaker imply when he says, "I'm afraid that only six people can join the program"?
(A) Not everyone can join the program.
(B) The speaker wants to buy a product.
(C) Employees need to move desks and shelves.
(D) The speaker will attend a ceremony.
Ⓐ Ⓑ Ⓒ Ⓓ

Reading Section

Let's Learn!

Part 5 短文穴埋め問題 ―受動態―

受動態の一般的な動詞の形は「be 動詞＋過去分詞」です。
能動態（～する）： This author **wrote** many books.
（この著者は多くの本を書きました）
受動態（～される）： Many books **were written** by this author.
（多くの本がこの著者によって書かれました）

（　　　）のうち正しいものを選びましょう。

1. The meeting was (hold / held) online yesterday.
2. Everyone is (encouraging / encouraged) to attend the ceremony.
3. We are going to (celebrate / be celebrated) our 10th anniversary next year.
4. All the equipment has (checked / been checked) before the launch.

Part 7 読解問題 文書の種類―広告②（advertisement）―

広告では、商品、サービス、イベント、セール、店のオープンなどを宣伝します。

広告を見て、下の問題の（　　）のうち正しいものを選びましょう。

Heavenly Hosts has everything you need for your next formal event! Our beautiful location is perfect for weddings, anniversary parties, or any company event. Call us at 555-9284 to talk to a representative.

1. どんなサービスの宣伝ですか。（イベント会場 / ウェディングドレス製作）
2. ここで何ができますか。（スポーツの試合 / パーティー）
3. 読み手は何をすべきですか。（電話をする / 会場に行く）

Let's Try!

Part 5 短文穴埋め問題

それぞれの空所に入れるのに最も適切なものを１つずつ選びましょう。

14. An award ------- to Mr. Alverez at the ceremony last month.
(A) give
(B) gave
(C) was given
(D) given
Ⓐ Ⓑ Ⓒ Ⓓ

15. All employees are encouraged to attend the -------.
(A) ceremony
(B) store
(C) accommodation
(D) destination
Ⓐ Ⓑ Ⓒ Ⓓ

16. Please note that the training session will ------- in the Conference Room A.
(A) hold
(B) be held
(C) be holding
(D) are held
Ⓐ Ⓑ Ⓒ Ⓓ

17. Kitts Co. is going ------- its 50th anniversary next year.
(A) celebrated
(B) has celebrated
(C) been celebrated
(D) to celebrate
Ⓐ Ⓑ Ⓒ Ⓓ

18. Be sure to check the audio equipment ------- the launch event.
(A) with
(B) under
(C) before
(D) between
Ⓐ Ⓑ Ⓒ Ⓓ

19. Many participants ------- at Ms. Jansenn's retirement party.
(A) came
(B) went
(C) gathered
(D) attended
Ⓐ Ⓑ Ⓒ Ⓓ

Part 6 長文穴埋め問題

それぞれの空所に入れるのに最も適切なものを１つずつ選びましょう。

Questions 20-23 refer to the following notice.

Thank you for 20 years!

Rangicorp has now been in business for 20 years! To celebrate our -------(**20.**), we updated the design of our award-winning refrigerators. The new products -------(**21.**) displayed at a launch event next month. All of our products will be available -------(**22.**) a special price during this promotion. -------(**23.**). We are sure you will love them!

20. (A) conference
(B) anniversary
(C) inventory
(D) participant

Ⓐ Ⓑ Ⓒ Ⓓ

21. (A) is
(B) are
(C) were
(D) will be

Ⓐ Ⓑ Ⓒ Ⓓ

22. (A) by
(B) with
(C) for
(D) on

Ⓐ Ⓑ Ⓒ Ⓓ

23. (A) Please note that the campus shuttle is delayed.
(B) Passengers can ask the driver about the route.
(C) Candidates are required to send a résumé.
(D) Customers are encouraged to visit us and see the exciting changes.

Ⓐ Ⓑ Ⓒ Ⓓ

Part 7 読解問題

文章を読んで、それぞれの設問の答えとして最も適切なものを１つずつ選びましょう。

Questions 24-26 refer to the following advertisement.

Heavenly Hosts

– [1] – Heavenly Hosts has everything you need for your next formal event! Our beautiful location is perfect for weddings, anniversary parties, award banquets, or any company event. – [2] – Our team can organize many types of ceremonies and will give participants detailed programs. – [3] – Let our caterers create a buffet or set menu for your guests. – [4] – We look forward to helping you make your next event special.

24. What type of business is Heavenly Hosts?
(A) An art museum
(B) A real estate agent
(C) A delivery company
(D) An event planner

Ⓐ Ⓑ Ⓒ Ⓓ

25. What is indicated about food?
(A) Guests can order anything.
(B) Participants must bring their own food.
(C) Buffets and set menus are available.
(D) No food is allowed in the ceremony hall.

Ⓐ Ⓑ Ⓒ Ⓓ

26. In which of the positions marked [1], [2], [3], and [4] does the following sentence best belong?

"Call us at 555-9284 to talk to a representative."
(A) [1]
(B) [2]
(C) [3]
(D) [4]

Ⓐ Ⓑ Ⓒ Ⓓ

Health

健康

Word Bank

次のボキャブラリーの日本語の意味を(　　)内に書き、下のイラストのアルファベットを[　　]内に入れましょう。

① facility (　　　　　　) [　　　]
② appointment (　　　　　　) [　　　]
③ fitness (　　　　　　) [　　　]
④ membership (　　　　　　) [　　　]
⑤ instructor (　　　　　　) [　　　]
⑥ patient (　　　　　　) [　　　]
⑦ exercise (　　　　　　) [　　　]
⑧ clinic (　　　　　　) [　　　]
⑨ pharmacy (　　　　　　) [　　　]
⑩ diet (　　　　　　) [　　　]

Listening Section

Let's Learn!

Part 2 応答問題 ―同じ発音・似た発音の語（句）―

最初の発話に含まれる語（句）と同じ発音や似た発音の語（句）が、正答以外の選択肢に含まれることがよくあります。これらを選ばないようにしましょう。
同じ発音の例：pair / pear, new / knew
似た発音の例：light / right, appointment / apartment

最初の発話に対する2つの応答a, bを読み、正しい応答を選びましょう。

1. I like the new fitness center. （　）
a. Me too. b. I knew that patient.

2. Please check your appointment. （　）
a. OK, I will. b. I don't live in the apartment.

3. Turn right at the corner by the pharmacy. （　）
a. OK, thanks. b. At the traffic light.

Part 3 会話問題 図表問題

Part 3 の最後には、図表を見ながら会話を聞いて答える問題が含まれます。図表問題は Look at the graphic.（図表を見てください）で始まります。

電話での会話文と表を見て、以下の問題に答えましょう。

Woman: Barton Gym, may I help you?
Man: I'm calling about your membership program. Are exercise classes included?
Woman: With our premium membership, clients can take fitness classes, but classes are not included in our other plans.
Man: I see.

Membership Rates	
Premium	€60/month
Standard	€40/month
Value	€20/month

1. 男性が知りたいことはなんですか。 a. ジムの会員制度 b. レストランの場所

2. 図表を見てください。フィットネスのクラスを含む会員の月謝はいくらですか。
a. 60 ユーロ b. 20 ユーロ

Let's Try!

Part 1 写真描写問題

2-62, 63

それぞれの写真について、4つの説明文のうち適切なものを1つずつ選びましょう。

1.

Ⓐ Ⓑ Ⓒ Ⓓ

2.

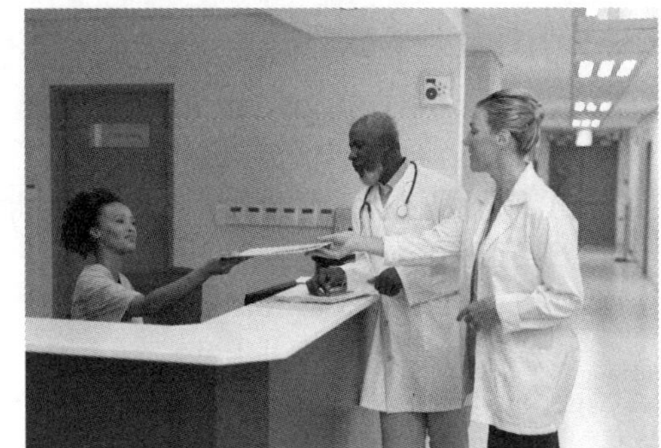

Ⓐ Ⓑ Ⓒ Ⓓ

Part 2 応答問題

2-64~68

それぞれの質問の応答として最も適切なものを1つずつ選びましょう。

3. Mark your answer on your answer sheet. Ⓐ Ⓑ Ⓒ

4. Mark your answer on your answer sheet. Ⓐ Ⓑ Ⓒ

5. Mark your answer on your answer sheet. Ⓐ Ⓑ Ⓒ

6. Mark your answer on your answer sheet. Ⓐ Ⓑ Ⓒ

7. Mark your answer on your answer sheet. Ⓐ Ⓑ Ⓒ

Part 3 会話問題

会話についての設問に対し、最も適切なものを１つずつ選びましょう。

Membership Rates	
Premium	$75/month
Standard	$60/month
Value	$45/month
1-day pass	$15

8. What is the purpose of the man's telephone call?
(A) To ask about a gym membership
(B) To sign up for a workshop
(C) To complain about a product
(D) To buy theater tickets
Ⓐ Ⓑ Ⓒ Ⓓ

9. Look at the graphic. How much does a membership with fitness classes cost?
(A) $15
(B) $45 per month
(C) $60 per month
(D) $75 per month
Ⓐ Ⓑ Ⓒ Ⓓ

10. What does the woman suggest that the man do?
(A) Read a brochure
(B) Send a payment
(C) Complete an application
(D) Make an appointment
Ⓐ Ⓑ Ⓒ Ⓓ

Part 4 説明文問題

説明文についての設問に対し、最も適切なものを１つずつ選びましょう。

11. What is the main purpose of the broadcast?
(A) To describe a college
(B) To announce a new hospital facility
(C) To explain a job requirement
(D) To advertise a pharmacy
Ⓐ Ⓑ Ⓒ Ⓓ

12. What services are provided?
(A) A free shuttle
(B) Fast delivery
(C) Product promotion
(D) Diet and exercise advice
Ⓐ Ⓑ Ⓒ Ⓓ

13. When can patients make appointments?
(A) Today
(B) This week
(C) Next week
(D) Next month
Ⓐ Ⓑ Ⓒ Ⓓ

Reading Section

Let's Learn!

Part 5 短文穴埋め問題　接続詞③—ペアになる語句—

2つの語句が対（ペア）になる表現を、相関語句と呼びます。
例：both A and B　※下線部が相関語句

（　　　）に入る正しい選択肢を選びましょう。

1. both A (　　) B　　(and / or / nor / but also)
2. either A (　　) B　　(and / or / nor / but also)
3. neither A (　　) B　　(and / or / nor / but also)
4. not only A (　　) B　　(and / or / nor / but also)

Part 7 読解問題　文書の種類—お知らせ②（notice / announcement）—

お知らせでは、主に告知、案内、警告、注意などが伝えられます。

お知らせを見て、下の問題の（　　）のうち正しいものを選びましょう。

Adventa Allergy Clinic Now Open!

We are pleased to announce that renovations to the building at our new location are complete. Adventa Allergy Clinic is in an amazing new facility with all of the latest equipment. If you think you have an allergy, we suggest that you make an appointment with one of our caring doctors.

1. このお知らせの話題は何ですか。　（クリニックの開業 / 改装工事）
2. 新しい場所の特徴は何ですか。　（最新の機器 / 美しい待合室）
3. 読み手は何をすべきですか。　（予約をする / 見学をする）

Let's Try!

Part 5 短文穴埋め問題

それぞれの空所に入れるのに最も適切なものを１つずつ選びましょう。

14. We recommend that you attend a training session ------- today or tomorrow.
(A) not only
(B) both
(C) neither
(D) either
Ⓐ Ⓑ Ⓒ Ⓓ

15. We are happy to inform you that we hired not only two yoga instructors ------- also a diet advisor.
(A) and
(B) but
(C) or
(D) yet
Ⓐ Ⓑ Ⓒ Ⓓ

16. Be sure to make ------- before visiting the doctor.
(A) an application
(B) a booking
(C) a reservation
(D) an appointment
Ⓐ Ⓑ Ⓒ Ⓓ

17. We ------- that you make a healthy meal plan with your gym instructor.
(A) teach
(B) recommend
(C) call
(D) close
Ⓐ Ⓑ Ⓒ Ⓓ

18. Ms. Delany will have to ------- her membership at Central Fitness Gym next month.
(A) renew
(B) renewed
(C) renewing
(D) having renewed
Ⓐ Ⓑ Ⓒ Ⓓ

19. We suggest that you ------- daily exercises at our fitness center.
(A) go
(B) play
(C) listen
(D) do
Ⓐ Ⓑ Ⓒ Ⓓ

Part 6 長文穴埋め問題

それぞれの空所に入れるのに最も適切なものを１つずつ選びましょう。

Questions 20-23 refer to the following article.

Fitness with Friends

A new study by researchers at Gorton University found that people who attend fitness classes continue ------- (20.) exercise longer than people who exercise alone. The researchers said that fitness instructors motivate their clients. -------. (21.) This helps them to exercise even when they really want to stay home. Beginners are ------- (22.) to start slowly and add more classes later. Many gyms offer fitness classes at their ------- (23.) and welcome new members.

20. (A) to
(B) by
(C) in
(D) for

Ⓐ Ⓑ Ⓒ Ⓓ

21. (A) However, participants will get a certificate.
(B) As a result, customers can buy new products at the pharmacy.
(C) Employees should be sure to attend the conference.
(D) In addition, when people make an appointment to meet others for exercise, they want to keep their promises.

Ⓐ Ⓑ Ⓒ Ⓓ

22. (A) encourage
(B) encouraging
(C) encouraged
(D) encourages

Ⓐ Ⓑ Ⓒ Ⓓ

23. (A) ceremonies
(B) facilities
(C) memberships
(D) representatives

Ⓐ Ⓑ Ⓒ Ⓓ

Part 7 読解問題

文章を読んで、それぞれの設問の答えとして最も適切なものを１つずつ選びましょう。

Questions 24-28 refer to the following announcement, notice, and Web page.

Adventa Allergy Clinic Now Open!

We are pleased to announce that renovations to the building at our new location are complete. Adventa Allergy Clinic is in an amazing new facility with all of the latest equipment. There is a pharmacy only twenty metres away, so it is very convenient for patients. If you think you have an allergy, we suggest that you make an appointment with one of our caring doctors. We look forward to helping the neighbourhood residents feel healthy!

In a multicultural city like Vancouver, there are people who come here from around the world. To help everyone get the best care possible, we have doctors who speak different languages on staff. Patients are encouraged to make an appointment with a doctor who speaks their language.

Diane Park
Chief Doctor,
Adventa Allergy Clinic

Home | Doctors | Information | Access

Adventa Clinic Doctors

Names:	Languages:	Available Days:
Dr. Shen Gaoyang	English and Chinese	Tuesday through Friday
Dr. Kate Kobayashi	English and Japanese	Monday, Wednesday through Friday
Dr. Diane Park	English and Korean	Monday through Thursday
Dr. Nelson Debois	English and French	Monday, Tuesday, Thursday, Friday

24. What is the purpose of the announcement?
(A) To report a delay
(B) To describe a festival
(C) To explain a diet
(D) To advertise a new clinic

Ⓐ Ⓑ Ⓒ Ⓓ

25. What is indicated about the pharmacy?
(A) It is very large.
(B) It is under construction.
(C) It is close to the clinic.
(D) It is a small branch.

Ⓐ Ⓑ Ⓒ Ⓓ

26. According to the announcement, what should people with allergies do?
(A) Use eye drops
(B) Take medicine
(C) Wear a mask
(D) Make an appointment

Ⓐ Ⓑ Ⓒ Ⓓ

27. Where is the clinic located?
(A) In a quiet neighbourhood
(B) In an international airport
(C) In a city where people from different cultures live
(D) In a mountain village twenty kilometers away from the city

28. Which day of the week is the chief doctor NOT available to talk to patients?
(A) Monday
(B) Tuesday
(C) Wednesday
(D) Friday

TEXT PRODUCTION STAFF

edited by　編集
Eiichi Tamura　田村 栄一
Yasutaka Sano　佐野 泰孝

cover design by　表紙デザイン
Nobuyoshi Fujino　藤野伸芳

CD PRODUCTION STAFF

recorded by　吹き込み者
Jack Merluzzi (AmE)　ジャック・マルージー（アメリカ英語）
Adelia Falk (AmE)　アデリア・ファルク（アメリカ英語）
Jon Madryj (CanE)　ジョン・マドレー（カナダ英語）
Nadia Mckechnie (BrE)　ナディア・マケックニー（イギリス英語）
Stuart O (AusE)　スチュアート・オー（オーストラリア英語）

AN AMAZING AVENUE FOR THE TOEIC® L&R TEST 400
頻出表現と頻出単語でつかむTOEIC® L&R TEST 400点

2024年1月10日　初版発行
2024年2月15日　第2刷発行

編著者　薭 寛美　Adelia Falk　福井 美奈子　衛藤 圭一
　　　　ラムスデン 多夏子　金田 直子　倉田 誠

発行者　佐野 英一郎

発行所　株式会社 成 美 堂
〒101-0052東京都千代田区神田小川町3-22
TEL 03-3291-2261　FAX 03-3293-5490
https://www.seibido.co.jp

印刷・製本　萩原印刷株式会社

ISBN 978-4-7919-7290-6　Printed in Japan

コア表現リスト　リスニング編

Listening

1	I'm calling to ～ / about ～ / because ～	～するために / ～の件で / ～なので 電話をしています
2	Why don't you ～	～してはどうですか
3	I'd like to remind you that ～	再度～をお知らせします
4	I was wondering if you could ～	～していただけませんか
5	I am / We are pleased to announce that ～	～をお知らせすることをうれしく思います
6	I'm having trouble -ing ～	～するのに困っています
7	Please remember to ～	～することを覚えておいてください
8	be available	入手可能です
9	I'm afraid that ～	残念ながら～です
10	We ask that you ～	～していただきますようお願いします
11	You (will) need to ～	～する必要があります
12	I want to let you know that ～	～をお知らせしたいと思います
13	Would you mind -ing ～	～していただけませんか
14	I / We would like to ～	～したいです

No.1 ～ 7　　ほぼ確実に設問の正答箇所となる
No.8 ～ 14　非常に高い確率で設問の正答箇所となる